# 0 To A Million In The Stock Market

## Journey To Financial Freedom

**Author: Dong Doan**

# Introduction

This book will provide the information and education for beginner investors. I do not offer advisory or brokerage services, nor does it recommend or advise investors to buy or sell particular stocks or securities that is mention in this book. This book will go over situation on how different type of investing can cause you to go from 0 dollar to 1 million dollar and that amount of time needing to do it. Will also break down on what each item are when you are looking at the stocks.

The first thing you need to understand is that finance is all about information. If you want to learn, you need to take in information. All of the information. Books, news, financial statements, press releases and earning calls. Read everything. You will find hundreds of words you don't understand, so look them up. In the beginning you will struggle, however, as time goes by, you will start to understand. If you do not like reading, learn to like it. There is no way around this. If you find yourself investing without reading tons, you are going to lose. In this book you will find everything you need about investing. What does investing mean and how does it work. Types of investments. Guidelines and mistake for beginner investors.
The stock market presents an almost unlimited opportunity to grow wealth by providing you with the opportunity to buy into any company of choice. Over the years, a lot of people have become rich by investing in the stock market. It would be great if you could follow in their footsteps!

# Chapter One

# The Stock Market

"The stock market is a device for transferring money from the impatient to the patient." –
Warren Buffett

When it comes to investing, we want our money to grow with the highest rates of return, and the lowest risk possible. While there are no shortcuts to getting rich, there are smart ways to go about it. One of the ways to get rich is by investing your money in the stock market.

The stock market is the collection of all companies that have shares of stock available for investors to purchase. You don't actually invest in the stock market, you invest in companies who are a part of it.

When you buy a share of stock, you are investing a set dollar amount into the company, which said company can use however they wish. In exchange, you now own a certain percentage of the company. This percentage does not change unless you buy or sell more stocks. As the company's overall value fluctuates, the value of your share also fluctuates. As the company starts doing well, your share of stock grows. The important thing to note, however, is that this means absolutely nothing to your total wealth until you sell the share. The only way to make money off the stock market is to sell your stock at a point when the company has more value than when you bought the stock, and the only way to lose money is by selling a stock when the company is worth less. You can lose money, because an investment is not a guarantee. You have to watch it mature, and potentially sell it if you think it's going to start losing value. But the important thing to remember is that you don't gain or lose anything until the moment you sell your stock.

## What Is The Difference Between Stocks And The Stock Market:
** Part One : Stocks **

First, let's imagine that down the street there is a toy store. Mr. Jones owns the toy store, and he has owned it for the last ten years. The toy store is a company which sells toys and all the kids love to get toys from Mr. Jones' toy store.

Let's suppose we wanted to buy Mr. Jones' toy store from him so that all of the kids would buy toys from us instead. Would we be able to buy it for a dollar? No, of course not. It is worth a lot more than that. How about ten dollars? A hundred dollars?

Well, how exactly would we find out how much we need to pay in order to buy Mr. Jones' toy store? The most important thing to consider is simply how much money is the toy store making. If the toy store is making $100 every day, that means it is making roughly $3,000 (30 days of $100) every month, or $36,000 every year (12 months of $3,000). Let's suppose we are able to figure that the toy store should be able to keep making this much for the next ten years. Then we could consider that the entire toy store is worth $360,000 (which is $36,000 for ten years).Now, in practice this is a lot more complicated. But the basic principle is simply to figure out how much money a company can be expected to make in a certain time frame. Fortunately, we don't have to figure it out ourselves. There are big companies whose job is to figure out how much other companies are worth, and they do all of the hard work for us. They will tell us just how much Mr. Jones' toy store is really worth, and then we can decide to buy it or not.

So, let's consider that the toy store is worth $360,000. If we want to buy it (and if he is willing to sell it), we can pay Mr. Jones that much money and now the toy store is ours!

Now, this is all well and good if we have $360,000 and we want to own the entire company. But let's suppose we only have half that much, we have $180,000. What can we do now? Well, as long as Mr. Jones is willing, we can buy half of his company instead of the whole thing.

This means that we will own 50% or half of the company, and he will own the other half. That means that instead of all of the money from selling toys going to Mr. Jones, half will go to him and the other half to us.

Another way of saying that we own 50% of the company is to say that we own 50% of the stock in a company. When a company is set up in a way that you can buy pieces of it, those pieces are called stock. There are two ways to think about stock: percentages, and shares.

What we just talked about are percentages. We can buy 50% of the shares in Mr. Jones' toy company for $180,000. Similarly, we could buy 10% of the shares in Mr. Jones' toy company for $36,000 (assuming the total value of the company was $360,000), or we could buy 1% of the shares for $3,600, and so on.

When you hear people talk about stocks, you will hear them talk about shares of stock. What exactly does this mean? Well, let's imagine that Mr. Jones has a lot of people who want to buy a piece of his company. What he can do is say "Hey everyone, I have 100 different pieces of my company for sale."

In this example, there are 100 total pieces he has for sale, each one being worth 1% of the stock. To buy all 100 pieces would cost you $360,000 and this would mean you own the entire company. This would mean that whenever the company makes money, you get all of the money. But let's suppose we only have $3,600 to use. This means all we can afford is one piece of his company, but that one piece is worth 1% which means that every time the company makes a hundred dollars, we will get one dollar.

So in this example, Mr. Jones' looks at the situation and realizes it is very hard to find people to buy pieces of his company, because each piece costs $3,600 which is a lot of money. So he decides rather than just have 100 pieces, or shares, he is going to have a thousand pieces! Now it takes ten shares to have 1% of the company, but each share is only $360. That is a lot 7more affordable. He could even decide to make 10,000 shares which means that you could buy a share for only $36.

So this is the basic concept. Companies cut their value into pieces, or shares, and then sell the shares to people who will buy them. The people who buy shares are called "investors" and the act of buying a share is called "investing". This means that they are buying shares in a company

because they think that eventually they will make back more than what they paid, because they are getting a piece of all of the money that the company makes.

When a company is enormous, worth billions of dollars, even a thousand shares is simply not enough. They need to have many, many shares in order to make sure that shares are affordable. Some companies have millions of shares of stock.

Now, we have covered one aspect of what it means to own stock in a company. You are able to keep some of the money the company makes, based on how many shares you own. But when you own part of a company, you don't just get some of the money it makes. You also get to make decisions. Everyone who has shares in a company has the right to vote for what the company will do next. The amount of voting power you have is equal to the percentage of shares you have.

Imagine that a company is owned by three people: Billy, Melissa, and James. Imagine that Billy owns 40% of the total shares, and that Melissa and James each own 30%, which is less than what Billy owns.
Let's suppose that the toy company is trying to decide whether to sell a certain toy. Billy thinks it is a good idea, but Melissa and James think it is a bad idea. Well, even though Billy has more shares of stock in the company, and more voting power, he will still be out voted by both Melissa and James. This is because together Melissa and James have 60% compared to Billy's 40%.

When a company has a lot of share holders (people who own stock in the company), they will have meetings called shareholder meetings. In these meetings, everyone gets to vote based on the shares they own. The company will do whatever the prevailing vote decides.
So then, this brings up a question. What if there are a lot of people who own shares, but one of them owns more than half of all the shares? Would that person be able to out-vote everyone else, no matter how many other people there are?

The answer is yes. If a single person owns more than half of all the shares, then they have what is called "controlling interest" in the company. This means that they can decide anything for the company and outvote everyone else.

** Part Two : The Stock Market **

So by now you should have a pretty good idea of what stock is. Now let's imagine that there is also a video game company owned by Mr. Smith. Now, Mr. Smith's company is doing a lot better than Mr. Jones'. We had said that Mr. Jones' company is worth $360,000 based on how much it is expected to make over ten years, but Mr. Smith's is worth twice that! His video game company is worth $720,000.

Let's imagine that Mr. Jones' company has 100 total shares of stock, each valued at $3,600 per share. Let's also imagine that Mr. Smith's company also has 100 total shares of stock, each valued at $7,200 per share. This means that if we had $7,200 we could choose to either buy two shares in Mr. Jones' toy company, or one share in Mr. Smith's video game company.

Let's suppose that we already own two shares of stock in Mr. Jones' toy company. Our two shares are worth $7,200 which is enough to buy one share of stock in Mr. Smith's company. We looked at both companies, and we decided that Mr. Smith's company seems like it is doing the best, so we decide to sell our two shares in Mr. Jones' toy company, and buy one share of stock in Mr. Smith's company. And this is the basics of stock trading.

Now here is where things get interesting. How much a company is really worth changes constantly. Mr. Jones' company has been making $100 every day for ten years, but all of last year his company was only making $50 per day! Is it still worth $360,000 ? Maybe it is losing value, or maybe it is just going through a rough period. If we owned stock in the company, we would have to decide which it is. If we decide the company is losing value, then we will probably want to sell our stocks and buy stocks in a company that is doing better.

There are a lot of reasons to assume that a company is doing better, or worse. We might have heard a rumor that Mr. Jones' toy company, even though it has only been making $50/day is about to start selling a really, really cool toy. We say "Wow, if he sells that toy lots of kids will buy it!" and so we decide to buy a lot of stock because we think that the stock is actually worth more than Mr. Jones says.

Similarly, we might have heard a rumor that an even better toy company is going to be opening up a store right next door to Mr. Jones' toy store. In this case, we might say "Oh no, we have a lot of shares of stock in Mr. Jones' toy company, and we better sell it fast! If we don't, we will lose money because the kids will all shop at the new toy store instead." You can see that emotion plays a big role in this.

Now let's imagine that instead of two companies (Mr. Jones' Toy Company, and Mr. Smith's Video Game Company), there are hundreds of companies. Let's also imagine there are thousands of people all trading stock in each company at the same time. Now you have what is called a stock exchange. If you take the value of all of the companies and add them together, and then divide that by the total number of companies in your stock exchange, you get an average that you can track over time to see how well on average all of the companies are doing.

Let's suppose that all of the companies combined are worth a million dollars, and that there are only ten total companies in the stock exchange. Then we would say that the average value is a million divided by ten which is $100,000. Remember though that how much companies are worth changes over time, so the very next day it might turn out that all ten companies combined are now worth two million dollars, which means our average is now $200,000.

If we keep track of this average over time, we can create a graph. We can watch this graph to get a good feel for how the companies in the stock exchange are doing. This can also help us decide whether or not investing in more companies is a good idea, or a bad idea.

## What is a ticker symbol?

A ticker symbol is a short version of the company that you can type in that's listed on the stock market. So for example, if you are trading McDonald's, instead of writing out the whole McDonald's name, the ticker symbol for McDonald's would be something like MCD so that way you know what your order is. There is only one company that owns that unique ticker symbol so you can't have like five different companies have MCD. They are assigned a specific ticker symbol right here for the trading community so for the Dow Jones, for the Nasdaq whatever index they're trading on, they're assigned that specific name. So if you have Facebook for example some of them are easy to remember some of them are a pain. You have FB, that's Facebook's ticker symbol so if you want to purchase shares of Facebook you type in FB, that's what it is. If you want to do something like caterpillar that one is cat. I mean there's all kinds of tickers out there you know you have Google so all sorts basically ticker symbol is just an abbreviation of the company so you can type it out quicker so it has its own unique value because you might have multiple companies with the same name. It's really rare but there are a couple companies that may have a very similar name so they don't get confused, they're always using ticker symbols and it's also faster for trade executions so as you get better you'll be familiar with all the different ticker symbols like Verizon Microsoft all kinds of ticker symbols out there and sometimes you will have to look up the companies but basically that's what a ticker symbol is, it's an abbreviated version of the company.

Benefits of Ticker Symbols:

- Every ticker symbol is unique (some companies have similar names and this eliminates confusion)

- It is faster to type than a full company name

- Faster for trade executions

**What is the stock exchange?**

When a company has bigger and better dreams that require more capital but when they don't have that capital then the company directors could go to a bank and ask for a business loan. But there will be an interest, that's mandatory to pay for the loan amount that has been taken from the bank and that's why many companies are getting listed on a stock exchange to raise capital to the projects that they're planning to start and to extend their cash flow. Though getting listed on a stock exchange will allow the businesses to raise capital without any interest, not all the businesses are eligible to be listed on a stock exchange. To be listed on a stock exchange a business has to be registered as a private limited company. Then the company should have a minimum valuation that has been assessed and audited. Also the company's balance sheet has to be clean. After achieving the primary requirements to be eligible to get listed on a stock exchange the company can decide the share percentage that they want to list on the stock exchange. Usually in most cases, it's less than 49 percent of the entire share percentage of the company. After deciding on that the company can proceed with the initial public offering also known as IPO. In an IPO the stock exchange will allow the general public to make offers for the newly listed company for couple of trading days.

**New York Stock Exchange**

The New York Stock Exchange (NYSE) is by far the world's largest stock exchange by market capitalization.

The NYSE's opening and closing bells mark the beginning and the end of each trading day. The opening bell is rung at **9:30 am** ET to mark the start of the day's trading session. At **4 pm** ET the closing bell is rung and trading for the day stops.

**The New York Stock Exchange has two primary functions:**

> It provides a central marketplace for investors to buy and sell stock.
> It enables companies to list their shares and raise capital from interested investors.

**Nasdaq Stock Market**

The Nasdaq Stock Market, or simply NASDAQ, is the second-largest stock exchange in the world for investors looking to buy and sell shares of stock. NASDAQ was initially an acronym, NASDAQ, which stands for the National Association of Securities Dealers Automated Quotations.

It is mainly for US Technology stocks and tracks about 4000 stocks. When you hear about the Nasdaq 100, it makes up the 100 largest companies in the NASDAQ.

Since we are talking about stock exchanges, we might as well briefly explain the S&P 500. I am sure you hear about it often. By the way, S&P stands for Standard and Poor.

It represents the 500 largest companies listed on the NYSE or NASDAQ. Investors use it as one of the best representations of the US Stock Market and economy.

## What is the S&P 500?

The S&P 500 is an index that's compiled of the 500 kind of biggest stocks there are in the marketplace and basically people use it as a measure of how the stock market is doing. The S&P 500 is maintained by the U.S. Index Committee. All committee members are full-time professional members of S&P Dow Jones Indices' staff. The committee meets monthly. At each meeting, the Index Committee reviews pending corporate actions that may affect index constituents, statistics comparing the composition of the indices to the market, companies that are being considered as candidates for addition to an index, and any significant market event.

To be eligible for S&P 500 index inclusion, a company should be a U.S. company, have a market capitalization of at least USD 8.2 billion, be highly liquid, have a public float of at least 10% of its shares outstanding, and its most recent quarter's earnings and the sum of its trailing four consecutive.

### Another exchange is the Dow Jones.

The Dow Jones Industrial Average, Dow Jones, or simply the Dow, is a stock market index that measures the stock performance of 30 large companies listed on stock exchanges in the United States.

### What is index fund?

There are a number of stock (and bond) indexes that have been published. Among the more famous are the S&P 500 and the Dow Jones. These are just basically lists of stocks that have been chosen to represent the market or a specific subset of the market.

The S&P 500 index, for example, represents stocks from 500 of the largest US companies.

There are mutual funds and exchange traded funds that you can invest in that are based on one of these indexes. You can invest in a single mutual fund, called an index fund, and your money will in turn be invested in all (or a representative sample) of the stocks or bonds in the index.

So for a single investment action on your part, if you invest money in an S&P 500 index fund, you're really having your money invested in 500 of the largest US corporations. In one investment, you have managed to get broad diversification over a large part of the US stock market.

S&P 500 index funds are offered by a variety of financial institutions. The ones from Vanguard, Fidelity and Schwab are very large and very cheap for them to run, so you are in turn charged an extremely low fee to get all of this diversification.

# Chapter Two

# The Difference Types Of Stocks

A stock gives an individual a share of ownership in a company. Stocks, a common investment vehicle, are available in different categories. Many of them have similar characteristics, such as moving in the same direction. Some stock categories are better investments than others, and some can fit into multiple categories. Each category should help investors make better investment decisions.

## 7 Categories of Classifying stock

## Blue Chip Stocks

Blue chip stocks are shares in large, stable companies that are continually profitable. They grow slowly and their earnings are extremely dependable. These stocks are expensive but provide the lowest risk and have an established track record for earnings.

## Speculative Stocks

Startup companies with little financial history typically issue speculative stocks. These companies often develop new, untested products, or they explore untapped markets. This type of stock comes with a high amount of risk because many of these companies fail; but the potential to get a huge return makes them appealing to some investors. If the company is successful, the stock will grow in value and increase the investor's rate of return.

## Growth Stocks

Growth stocks are issued by companies that are expected to have high earnings. However, the earnings are reinvested back into the business to fund development. These stocks pay low dividends, if any. This doesn't deter some investors, because as the company grows, its stock value is likely to increase.

## Value Stocks

Value stocks are viewed as undervalued in the market, but investors see potential. The company that issues the stock has assets that are worth more than the stock price. Investors believe the company's shares are a bargain and will become more valuable in the future when the company's troubled industry improves, or the company grows.

## Income Stocks

Income stocks often are blue chip stocks from well-established companies. The stocks normally pay high dividends; at times this may include the majority of earnings. This is the least volatile class of stock that provides investors with a consistently growing income stream. Companies with this type of stock are usually in stable industries such as energy, finance, utilities and natural resources.

## Penny Stocks

Penny stocks are low-priced stocks with high risk. They trade at no more than $5 per share and sometimes as low as 2 cents a share. This type of stock typically is issued by small startups that need to make money. If the company does well, the stock's value can increase dramatically. However, most stocks in this category fail to thrive.

## Cyclical Stocks

Cyclical stocks are dependent on the health of the economy. During strong economic times, the stocks flourish. During tough economic times, they lose a substantial amount of value. The companies that issue these types of stocks can be found in the airline industry, electronics or car manufacturing.

## Different Types of Stocks

As you dive into researching stocks, you'll often hear them discussed with reference to different categories of stocks and different classifications. Here are the major types of stocks you should know.

1. Common stock

2. Preferred stock

3. Large-cap stocks

4. Mid-cap stocks

5. Small-cap stocks

6. Domestic stock

7. International stocks

8. Growth stocks

9. Value stocks

10. IPO stocks

11. Dividend stocks

12. Non-dividend stocks

13. Income stocks

14. Cyclical stocks stocks

15. Non-cyclical stocks

16. Safe stocks

17. ESG stocks

18. Blue chip stocks

19. Penny stocks

## Common stock and preferred stock

Most stock that people invest in its common stock. Common stock represents partial ownership in a company, with shareholders getting the right to receive a proportional share of the value of any remaining assets if the company gets dissolved. Common stock gives shareholders theoretically unlimited upside potential, but they also risk losing everything if the company fails without having any assets left over.

Preferred stock works differently, as it gives shareholders a preference over common shareholders to get back a certain amount of money if the company dissolves. Preferred shareholders also have the right to receive dividend payments before common shareholders do. The net result is that preferred stock as an investment often more closely resembles fixed-income bond investments than regular common stock. Often, a company will offer only common stock. This makes sense, as that is what shareholders most often seek to buy.

### Large-cap, mid-cap, and small-cap stocks

Stocks also get categorized by the total worth of all their shares, which is called market capitalization. Companies with the biggest market capitalizations are called large-cap stocks, with mid-cap and small-cap stocks representing successively smaller companies.

There's no precise line that separates these categories from each other. However, one often-used rule is that stocks with market capitalizations of $10 billion or more are treated as large-caps, with stocks having market caps between $2 billion and $10 billion qualifying as mid-caps and stocks with market caps below $2 billion getting treated as small-cap stocks.

Large-cap stocks are generally considered safer and more conservative as investments, while mid caps and small caps have greater capacity for future growth but are riskier. However, just because two companies fall into the same category here doesn't mean they have anything else in common as investments or that they'll perform in similar ways in the future.

Make your portfolio reflect your best vision for our future.

### Domestic stocks and international stocks

You can categorize stocks by where they're located. For purposes of distinguishing domestic U.S. stocks from international stocks, most investors look at the location of the company's official headquarters.

However, it's important to understand that a stock's geographical category doesn't necessarily correspond to where the company gets its sales. Philip Morris International (NYSE:PM) is a great example, as its headquarters are in the U.S., but it sells its tobacco and other products exclusively outside the country. Especially among large multinational corporations, it can be hard to tell from business operations and financial metrics whether a company is truly domestic or international.

## Growth stocks and value stocks

Another categorization method distinguishes between two popular investment methods. Growth investors tend to look for companies that are seeing their sales and profits rise quickly. Value investors look for companies whose shares are inexpensive, whether relative to their peers or to their own past stock price.

Growth stocks tend to have higher risk levels, but the potential returns can be extremely attractive. Successful growth stocks have businesses that tap into strong and rising demand among customers, especially in connection with longer-term trends throughout society that support the use of their products and services. Competition can be fierce, though, and if rivals disrupt a growth stock's business, it can fall from favor quickly. Sometimes, even just a growth slowdown is enough to send prices sharply lower, as investors fear that long-term growth potential is waning.

Value stocks, on the other hand, are seen as being more conservative investments. They're often mature, well-known companies that have already grown into industry leaders and therefore don't have as much room left to expand further. Yet with reliable business models that have stood the test of time, they can be good choices for those seeking more price stability while still getting some of the positives of exposure to stocks.

## IPO stocks

IPO stocks are stocks of companies that have recently gone public through an initial public offering. IPOs often generate a lot of excitement among investors looking to get in on the ground floor of a promising business concept. But they can also be volatile, especially when there's disagreement within the investment community about their prospects for growth and profit. A stock generally retains its status as an IPO stock for at least a year and for as long as two to four years after it becomes public.

## Dividend stocks and non-dividend stocks

Many stocks make dividend payments to their shareholders on a regular basis. Dividends provide valuable income for investors, and that makes dividend stocks highly sought after among certain investment circles.

However, stocks don't have to pay dividends. Non-dividend stocks can still be strong investments if their prices rise over time. Some of the biggest companies in the world don't pay dividends, although the trend in recent years has been toward more stocks making dividend payouts to their shareholders.

## Income stocks

Income stocks are another name for dividend stocks, as the income that most stocks pay out comes in the form of dividends. However, income stocks also refer to shares of companies that have more mature business models and have relatively fewer long-term opportunities for growth. Ideal for conservative investors who need to draw cash from their investment portfolios right now, income stocks are a favorite among those in or nearing retirement.

## Cyclical stocks and non-cyclical stocks

National economies tend to follow cycles of expansion and contraction, with periods of prosperity and recession. Certain businesses have greater exposure to broad business cycles, and investors therefore refer to them as cyclical stocks.

Cyclical stocks include shares of companies in industries like manufacturing, travel, and luxury goods, because an economic downturn can take away customers' ability to make major purchases quickly. When economies are strong, however, a rush of demand can make these companies rebound sharply.

By contrast, non-cyclical stocks, also known as secular or defensive stocks, don't have those big swings in demand. An example would be grocery store chains, because no matter how good or bad the economy is, people still have to eat. Non-cyclical stocks tend to perform better during market downturns, while cyclical stocks often outperform during strong bull markets.

## Safe stocks

Safe stocks are stocking whose share prices make relatively small movements up and down compared with the overall stock market. Also known as low-volatility stocks, safe stocks typically operate in industries that aren't as sensitive to changing economic conditions. They often pay dividends as well, and that income can offset falling share prices during tough times.

## Stock market sectors

You'll often see stocks broken down by the type of business they're in. The basic categories most often used include:

Communication Services -- telephone, internet, media, and entertainment companies

Consumer Discretionary -- retailers, automakers, and hotel and restaurant companies

Consumer Staples -- food, beverage, tobacco, and household and personal products companies

Energy -- oil and gas exploration and production companies, pipeline providers, and gas station operators

Financial -- banks, mortgage finance specialists, and insurance and brokerage companies

Healthcare -- health insurers, drug and biotech companies, and medical device makers

Industrial -- airline, aerospace and defense, construction, logistics, machinery, and railroad companies

Materials -- mining, forest products, construction materials, packaging, and chemical companies

Real Estate -- real estate investment trusts and real estate management and development companies

Technology -- hardware, software, semiconductor, communications equipment, and IT services companies

Utilities -- electric, natural gas, water, renewable energy, and multi-product utility companies

## ESG investing

ESG investing refers to an investment philosophy that puts emphasis on environmental, social, and governance concerns. Rather than focusing entirely on whether a company generates profit and is growing its revenue over time, ESG principles consider other collateral impacts on the environment, company employees, customers, and shareholder rights.

Tied to ESG's governing rules is socially responsible investing, or SRI. Investors using SRI screen out stocks of companies that don't match up to their most important values. However, ESG investing has a more positive element in that rather than just excluding companies that fail key tests, it actively encourages investing in the companies that do things the best. With evidence showing that a clear commitment to ESG principles can improve investing returns, there's a lot of interest in the area.

## Blue chip stocks and penny stocks

Finally, there are stock categories that make judgments based on perceived quality. Blue chip stocks tend to be the cream of the crop in the business world, featuring companies that lead their respective industries and have gained strong reputations. They typically don't provide the absolute highest returns, but their stability makes them favorites among investors with lower tolerance for risk.

By contrast, penny stocks are low-quality companies whose stock prices are extremely inexpensive, typically less than $1 per share. With dangerously speculative business models, penny stocks are prone to schemes that can drain your entire investment. It's important to know about the dangers of penny stocks.

# Index Funds VS Mutual Funds VS ETF

## Mutual funds

Mutual funds are investment strategies that allow you to pool your money together with other investors to purchase a collection of stock, bonds, or other securities. The value of the mutual fund company depends on the performance of the securities it decides to buy. Unlike stock, mutual fund shares do not give its holders any voting rights. A share of a mutual fund represents investments in many different stocks (or other securities) instead of just one holding. Mutual fund are typically actively manage.

Mutual Fund Fees

A mutual fund will classify expenses into either annual operating fees or shareholder fees. Annual fund operating fees are an annual percentage of the funds under management, usually ranging from 1–3%. Annual operating fees are collectively known as the expense ratio. A fund's expense ratio is the summation of the advisory or management fee and its administrative costs

Key Takeaways

> •A mutual fund is a type of investment vehicle consisting of a portfolio of stocks, bonds, or other securities.

•Mutual funds give small or individual investors access to diversified, professionally managed portfolios at a low price.

•Mutual funds are divided into several kinds of categories, representing the kinds of securities they invest in, their investment objectives, and the type of returns they seek.

•Mutual funds charge annual fees (called expense ratios) and, in some cases, commissions, which can affect their overall returns.

•The overwhelming majority of money in employer-sponsored retirement plans goes into mutual funds.

## Index Fund

An index fund creates a portfolio of stocks that mirror the collection of companies and performance of a market index, such as the S&P 500. Index funds are passively managed and have lower fees than actively managed funds, often generating higher investment returns

Index funds are generally considered ideal core portfolio holdings for retirement accounts, such as individual retirement accounts (IRAs) and 401(k) accounts. Legendary investor Warren Buffett has recommended index funds as a haven for savings for the later years of life. Rather than picking out individual stocks for investment, he has said, it makes more sense for the average investor to buy all of the S&P 500 companies at the low cost an index fund offers

Key Takeaways

- An index fund is a portfolio of stocks or bonds designed to mimic the composition and performance of a financial market index.

- Index funds have lower expenses and fees than actively managed funds.

- Index funds follow a passive investment strategy.

- Index funds seek to match the risk and return of the market, on the theory that in the long-term, the market will outperform any single investment.

## ETF (Exchange- traded funds)

Exchange-traded funds One of the most significant differences between an index fund and an ETFs is how they trade. Shares of ETFs trade like stocks; they're bought and sold whenever markets are open. While you can order index fund shares whenever you wish, share purchases only happen once a day, after the markets close. This means that the price of any given ETF fluctuates throughout the trading day, while the price of an index fund only changes once a day.

Key Takeaways

- An exchange traded fund (ETF) tracks a particular set of securities like an index; a stock ETF tracks a set of stocks.

- ETFs provide investors with immediate diversification within a low cost, easily tradeable vehicle.

- Research suggests that passive-investment vehicles like ETFs tend to return more than actively-managed vehicles like mutual funds over the long run

Target-Date Funds:

Index funds mirror the performance of a stock or bond index, often at a low cost. Expense ratios are usually at or below 0.1% for U.S. stock and bond index funds, and they can be less than 0.2% for international assets. However, investors are left on their own. They must put these assets together in ways that minimize risks for a given level of expected returns. That's great, as long as you're interested in modern portfolio theory (MPT).

Target-date funds can use both managed and index funds to create portfolios that professional managers believe are appropriate for investors. As the target date approaches, managers reduce the allocation to risky assets, such as international stocks, and increase the portion of funds dedicated to less volatile assets like bonds. Most of the best target-date funds have expense ratios of less than 1%, and some even go below 0.1%. As a rule, target-date funds that invest in index funds tend to charge less.

KEY TAKEAWAYS

- Index funds offer more choices and lower costs, while a target-date fund is an easy way to invest for retirement without worrying about asset allocations.

- Index funds include passively-managed exchange-traded funds (ETFs) and mutual funds that track specific indexes.

- Investors can combine index funds themselves to get performance similar to target-date funds and reduce fees in the process.

- Target-date funds are actively managed and periodically restructured to gradually reduce risk as the target retirement date approaches.

- Target-date funds can be riskier than most people expect, but they usually become less volatile than individual stock market index funds as the target date approaches.

## Chapter 4: Difference investing account

If you are just considering getting started investing, you may be overwhelmed by the first choice on the investment account application: what type of account do you want? The truth is that there are a lot of different accounts for different purposes. Knowing what type of investing account needs will help you guide where you want to place your money.

First, there are two main distinctions in accounts: brokerage and retirement. Brokerage accounts can be accessed at any time to deposit and withdraw funds. Retirement accounts have restrictions on how much can be invested annually and can usually only be withdrawn upon in retirement.

Both types also have their benefits. Brokerage accounts can invest in any investment product and can also take on leverage and short positions. Retirement accounts are somewhat limited in what they can invest in, but they usually offer some type of tax advantage.

### Brokerage Investment Accounts

Cash – A cash brokerage account is the most basic form of investment account. It's also known as a standard brokerage account. This account type is funded by your cash, and you can only invest with the cash in the account. This account is limited in what you can do because you can only use your cash. For example, you can't engage in certain options trading, and you can short sell either. If you're interested in that type of trading, you should look for a margin account. You should note that everything you do in a cash account is taxable, so make sure you pick your investments wisely.

Margin – A margin account is very similar to a cash account except you can trade on margin. This means that you're able to borrow from the brokerage when you place a trade. It still requires a certain amount of capital, and you can usually borrow up to 50% of what you have. A margin account gives you the ability to place every trade possible – including options trades and short selling. This is all since you're able to borrow from the broker to conduct the trade. Just like a cash account, a margin account is fully taxable.

### Retirement Investing Accounts

When it comes to saving for retirement, there are a lot of different investment vehicles. IRAs are the main type that you can go an open. You may be familiar with a 401k or 403b, but those are employer sponsored plans and individuals don't open those accounts.

Traditional IRA – A Traditional IRA (individual retirement account) is a savings vehicle that allows you to save and invest for retirement. The benefit of using a Traditional IRA is that, in many cases, the amount you contribute is tax deductible. Once you put money inside the account, everything you do or trade is tax deferred. You only pay taxes once you withdraw the money in retirement, but you will do so at ordinary income tax rates.

Roth IRA – A Roth IRA is like a Traditional IRA, except that you invest using after-tax money. Inside the account, both the Roth and Traditional IRA act the same. However, with the Roth IRA, when you withdraw your money in retirement, you don't pay any taxes on it. For these accounts, the gamble is this: do you think you're going to be in a higher tax bracket now or later. If you are paying higher taxes now, and think you'll pay less in retirement, a Traditional IRA makes sense because you get the tax breaks today. However, if you are in a low tax bracket now and plan to be in a higher tax bracket in retirement, a Roth IRA is the better choice.

**There are four basic types of investment accounts:**

> 1. Individual Brokerage Account (or Joint Brokerage Account)

2. IRA (Individual Retirement Account): Roth or Traditional

3. 401k, 403b and SEP

4. 529 College Savings Account

## 1. Individual Brokerage Account

An individual brokerage account is the most basic and flexible type of investment account. In the simplest terms, a brokerage account allows you to buy and sell investment vehicles through a licensed broker with very little restrictions.

Opening an individual brokerage account has become very simple thanks to the rise of online brokers. The basic process is as follows:

1. Open an online brokerage account

2. Deposit money into the account – there are a couple ways to do this, but the easiest is to link your checking account and electronically transfer money. You can usually mail a check as well if you prefer.

3. Start Investing

### Key Benefits:

•No contribution limits

•No restrictions on withdrawing funds

Drawbacks:

•Taxed on the way in

•Taxed on the way out

Note: I will use the above terminology in the rest of this post on types of investment accounts, the definitions are below:

•Taxed on the way in: Your money is taxed when you earn it (state and federal taxes on your income / checks from work).

•Taxed on the way out: Your money is taxed as you withdraw it from your investment accounts. Note, for most accounts (excluding Traditional IRAs and 401ks) this only applies to capital gains and not the money you initially contributed. Two quick examples to help illustrate:•You buy Apple stock for $1,000, sell it for $2,000, and are taxed on the capital gains of $1,000.

•You contribute $1,000 to your 401k pre-tax (into various investments). It grows to $2,000 when you retire. Taxation occurs on the full $2,000 when you withdraw it.

Types of investment accounts - tax

**Joint Brokerage Account**

A brokerage account shared with another individual is a joint brokerage account. For example, your spouse.

## 2. IRA

An account designed to help you save for retirement is an IRA (Individual Retirement Account) – exactly what it sounds like. There are significant tax benefits to IRAs that help you keep more of your money, but also some rules on when you can withdraw your money (and penalties if you do not follow these rules).

Tax-advantaged accounts come with rules you need to follow. Here a couple key ones to keep in mind with IRAs:

•Max Contributions: In 2021, the maximum amount of money you can contribute to an IRA is $6,000 ($7,000 if you are 50+ using catch up contributions) annually. This applies to both Roth and Traditional IRAs (so, you cannot contribute $6,000 each to both a Roth and Traditional IRA).

•Withdrawal Rules:  Money withdrawn before age 59.5 has a 10% additional tax (note: for Roth IRAs this only applies to capital gains, not your original contribution).

•Income Limits (Roth): Your ability to contribute to a Roth IRA reduces (and eventually goes down to $0) if your modified adjusted gross income (MAGI) is above certain levels. If you are single or filing separately from your spouse, the limit is $125,000. If you are married filing jointly the limit is $198,000.

•Income Limits (Traditional): For a traditional IRA, the limits depend on if you qualify for a retirement plan through work. If you do not qualify for a corporate-sponsored plan, then there are no income limits.

You can read more about IRAs rules here.

There are several types of IRAs, but the two most common are the Roth IRA and Traditional IRA.

**Roth IRA**

Roth IRAs are accounts that you put post-tax income into, but you can withdraw any capital gains tax-free when you retire. In other words, you get taxed now (by using post-tax income) and get the benefit later (when you pull your money out at retirement tax-free).

Key Benefits:

•Not taxed on the way out

•No mandatory withdrawals

•Can withdraw your contributions anytime (although not usually recommended, it is a good safety net)

Drawbacks:

•Contribution limits

•Penalty if capital gains withdrawal before age 59.5

•Taxed on the way in

## Traditional IRA

A Traditional IRA is an account that you contribute pre-tax income into*, but you get taxed on your contributions and capital gains when you withdraw. In other words, you benefit now (by using pre-tax income) and get taxed later (when you pull your money out at retirement).

Traditional IRAs operate very similarly to corporate sponsored 401ks in that they use pre-tax income.

*Technically you deduct your contributions when doing taxes.

Key Benefits:

•Not taxed on the way in

**Drawbacks:**

•Contribution limits (if you qualify for an employer-sponsored retirement plan)

•Penalty if withdrawal before age 59.5

•Mandatory withdrawals starting at age 72 (if you were born after June 30, 1949)

•Additional rules when also utilizing corporate-sponsored plan (I.e. 401k)

•Taxed on the way out

There are a lot of rules and drawbacks to keep in mind when dealing with these types of investment accounts, but do not let that scare you, IRAs are extremely useful tools in helping to save for retirement.

### 3. 401k, 403b and SEP

A 401k is a corporate-sponsored account provided by your employer. As mentioned above, a 401k is similar to a Traditional IRA – it offers a tax break on your income now and you are taxed on your money later. With 401ks, you designate a percent of your income (paycheck) that you want to contribute, and it is automatically deducted and invested for you.

The largest benefit of a 401k is employer match programs. In short, some companies contribute a certain percentage of your income to your 401k in addition to your contributions (as long as you meet certain contribution thresholds). The most common example is companies matching 50% of the first 6% you contribute.

**There are a few rules to keep in mind with 401ks:**

•Max Contributions: The max contribution for any individual is $19,500 annually, while the max contribution for the individual + employer is $58,000 annually.

•Withdrawal Rules: Money withdrawn before age 59.5 has a 10% additional tax.

•Mandatory Withdrawals: Similar to Traditional IRAs, you must start withdrawing from the plan starting at age 72 (if you were born after June 30, 1949)

Key Benefits:

•Not taxed on the way in

•Employer matching contributions

•Automatically deducted from paycheck

You can get 7 tips to maximize your 401(k) benefits here.

Drawbacks:

•Contribution limits

•Penalty if withdrawal before age 59.5

•Mandatory withdrawals starting age 70.5

•Taxed on the way out

•Limited investment vehicle options: typically, there are only a handful of mutual funds to choose from when investing in a 401k (versus the unlimited options when investing through a broker in an IRA or personal brokerage account)

Check out Blooom for a free 401(k) analysis to see if your account is set up as optimally as possible. Other, less common types of investment accounts offered by employers include:

•Pension Plans: Becoming rarer for corporations to offer, but arguably one of the best retirement plans for individuals out there.

•403b: Similar to a 401k, but typically utilized by public schools or non-profits.

•457: Similar to a 401k, but typically utilized by local and state governments (police officers, firefighters, etc.).

•Solo 401k: A 401k plan for sole proprietors.

•SEP IRA: IRA Plans for small businesses.

•Simple IRA: A simpler retirement account typically used by small businesses.

## 4. 529 College Savings Account

Last on the list of types of investment accounts is the 529 Savings Account. This account is designed to help save for a beneficiary's higher education and includes generous tax benefits.

Key Benefits:

•Not taxed on the way out

•Can use at most schools nationwide (not limited to certain states)

•Some states offer matching programs

Drawbacks:

•Limited to only use on education expenses for a beneficiary

•Taxed on the way in

## Which Type of Investment Account Should I Open?

If you are just getting started investing, and don't plan on accessing your investments until retirement, you should consider a retirement account. These accounts have lots of tax benefits and are designed for long term investment strategies.

Remember, an investment account is like a vehicle, while your actual investments are the passengers. Depending on the vehicle you own, it can only hold certain numbers and types of passengers. Plus, certain other rules will apply. That is how accounts work. Inside the account, you hold your stocks, bonds, mutual funds, etc. Some accounts have limits on how much you can put in, and there are rules about what types of investments you can hold in certain types of accounts. Depending on your situation will determine the account strategies with your money.

# Chapter Three

## Fundamentals

### How does a company get on the stock exchange?

Before a company gets on the stock exchange, it is considered a private company. This means that nobody is in your business. What happens in your business, stays in your business.  When a company decides to go public, everybody gets in their business. Going public means that they will need an Initial Public Offering or IPO. It's the process through which a privately held company offers shares to the public and begins trading on a stock exchange like the New York Stock Exchange or the Nasdaq.

An IPO company therefore is one that has filed to go public, declaring its intentions in a registration statement, or form S-1, with the Securities and Exchange Commission (SEC).

When a company is ready to go public, generally after it has a track record of growth and other favorable results, it hires an investment bank (or several banks) to come in and underwrite the IPO. That bank will then put up a sum of money to fund the IPO and agree to buy the shares being offered before they're actually listed on a public exchange.

The IPO company will file a registration statement, which includes its prospectus, providing detailed information on areas like its finances, results, business model, and growth opportunities. The underwriter must also perform due diligence on the IPO company to verify its financial information and analyze its business model and prospects.

Once all of the SEC's concerns have been addressed, the company often goes on an IPO roadshow to sell the stock to institutional investors. When the initial block of shares has been sold, or subscribed, the company and its underwriters set an initial price and date for the stock to begin trading.

On the first day of trading, the stock will become available to the general public as the underwriter sells shares on the stock market. Stocks often fluctuate wildly on opening day, as it's difficult to assess demand for newly public stocks, and it's not uncommon for a stock to double on opening day.

### Why would a company go public?

Before a company gets on the stock exchange, it is considered a private company. This means that nobody is in your business. What happens in your business, stays in your business. When a company decides to go public, everybody gets in their business. Going public means that they will need an Initial Public Offering or IPO. It's the process through which a privately held company offers shares to the public and begins trading on a stock exchange like the New York Stock Exchange or the Nasdaq.

An IPO company therefore is one that has filed to go public, declaring its intentions in a registration statement, or form S-1, with the Securities and Exchange Commission (SEC).

When a company is ready to go public, generally after it has a track record of growth and other favorable results, it hires an investment bank (or several banks) to come in and underwrite the IPO. That bank will then put up a sum of money to fund the IPO and agree to buy the shares being offered before they're actually listed on a public exchange.

The IPO company will file a registration statement, which includes its prospectus, providing detailed information on areas like its finances, results, business model, and growth opportunities. The underwriter must also perform due diligence on the IPO company to verify its financial information and analyze its business model and prospects.

Once all of the SEC's concerns have been addressed, the company often goes on an IPO roadshow to sell the stock to institutional investors. When the initial block of shares has been sold, or subscribed, the company and its underwriters set an initial price and date for the stock to begin trading.

On the first day of trading, the stock will become available to the general public as the underwriter sells shares on the stock market. Stocks often fluctuate wildly on opening day, as it's difficult to assess demand for newly public stocks, and it's not uncommon for a stock to double on opening day.

The primary benefit of going public is easier access to capital. The money a company raises can then be used for things such as expansion, research and development, marketing, or whatever else a company needs to grow or reach profitability. In addition to raising money, the IPO also rewards stakeholders in the company, such as employees, investors, founders, and others who own company stock but can't do much with it until that stock starts trading publicly. Once the stock is publicly traded, they can easily sell their holdings if they wish, generally after a lock-up period of six months that prevents insiders from dumping their stock immediately after the IPO.

Additionally, freed from the clunky process of private funding rounds, the stock has the potential to appreciate much faster than it would as a private company, assuming the business warrants it.

There are drawbacks to going public, however, as companies are required to adhere to SEC reporting guidelines, putting out regular disclosure statements and sharing their financial results, or opening up their books for all to see. Furthermore, a public company will also need to start answering to its shareholders, including in quarterly earnings calls. Those demands mean that management loses some control, as well as time and money, in exchange for that additional funding. Still, it's often a reasonable trade-off to make

## What is the company valuation?

For investors, company valuation is a critical component in determining the potential return on investment and if the company is "fairly valued" at the time of the investment. And for employees, company valuation is especially important if you're granted stock or stock options. A higher valuation might mean the options will increase in value.

Various company attributes must be considered to properly value the company. This includes vertical market and industry performance, proprietary technology or commodity, company operating experience, stage of growth, revenue & profitability growth, management team, and execution to plan.

There are also outside factors including comparable company performance, overall economic factors, market sentiment, and growth rate. When you add in the impact of technology (every company is influenced by technology) it becomes quite complex to come to a definitive equation.

**What is Market Cap:**

Market Cap is short for Market capitalization. it is calculated by multiplying a company's shares outstanding by the current market price of one share. Here, outstanding shares include stock owned by the public as well as restricted shares owned by the company's officials and employee.

There are 3 market capitalization factors:

- **Small Cap:**

Small cap stocks are usually the companies with less than 2 billion dollars. It is the starting point for all new companies. If valued under $2 billion, the company is in the small-cap category. But you have to note that small doesn't mean unimportant or a bad investment. You may even have heard of a handful of them, as this category can include restaurants, retail stores, product manufacturers, online companies and more.

- **Mid Cap:**

Mid-cap stocks are between 2 billion dollars and 10 million dollar. These companies that don't hit the threshold for large-cap. These middle companies are doing some big things. If you can buy one that's on track to change the world, you could find yourself with a huge investment gain. Look at the labels around your house and you're sure to find at least a few mid-cap brands.

- **Large Cap:**

Large-cap companies are the companies who have a 10 billion dollars or more market cap. That many people have heard of. But with no upper limit, it includes massive companies like Microsoft, Amazon, and Apple, each around the $1 trillion mark. That's why some analysts add a fourth category, mega-cap, for companies worth at least $200 billion.

**Financials:**
The best indicator for companies financials is their cash flow statement. Other financial documents (and stock price) can be misleading, but cash flows tell you everything.
All publicly traded companies (such as Netflix) are required to routinely publish financial statements,

including statement of cash flows. You can find them easily just by googling "Netflix financial statements" for example. the document doesn't do you a lot of good without a basic understanding of accounting/cash flow, balance sheet and the income statement. These reports are also sent out quarterly, so it's too soon to see any impact.

**Cash flows** tell you how specifically cash is coming in or out of the business. It tells you how much they gain or lose to operations, investing, and financing. You can also compare this statement to previous statements to see how their revenue and expenses are changing.

**Balance sheet** reports a company's assets, liabilities, and equity at a single moment in time. You can think of it like a snapshot of what the business looked like on that day in time. It does not report activities over a period of time. The balance sheet is essentially a picture a company's recourses, debts, and ownership on a given day. This is why the balance sheet is sometimes considered less reliable or less telling of a company's current financial performance than a profit and loss statement. Annual income statements look at performance over the course of 12 months, where as, the statement of financial position only focuses on the financial position of one day.

**Income statement** is a history book of the sales, costs, and expenses over a given period of time. Publicly traded companies are required to publish them. The Income Statement is one of a company's core financial statements that shows their profit and loss over a period of time.  The profit or loss is determined by taking all revenues and subtracting all expenses from both operating and non-operating activities

To calculate the income statement, you start by looking at the sales that have been made for that period, then subtract—in a series of stages—the costs and expenses of running the organization, beginning with the costs most closely associated with the sales.

Your top line reflects your sales, and your bottom line is however much money you have left after everything else has been taken into account. The income statement displays both of those numbers, as well as all the subtotals in between.

## Types Of Investments

There are multiple investment types, or asset classes, that you can choose from, each with distinct characteristics, risks and benefits.

- **Shares:** Investment in shares mean that you buy and keep the stock for a while in order to make money. If the company is growing and becomes more valuable, then the share worth more - so your investment is worth more too. A lot of shares pay you part of the company's profits each year, called a dividend.

- **Bonds:** bond is a contract where a company or government borrows money from a person for a period of time in return for interest payments. Think of it as a company or government taking out a loan directly from an individual. There are two kinds of bonds, Coupon and Zero coupon bonds. With coupon bonds the lender lends the set amount to the borrower and the borrower will make periodic payments to the lender and then return the money to the lender at the end of the term. A zero coupon bond is when the lender lends the set amount to the boarder, however they doesn't have to make payments but will return a larger amount to the lender at the end of the term.

- **Investment Funds:** the underlying principle is simply a group of investors perhaps thousands pull their money and invest in various assets, stocks and bonds amongst others. These pools otherwise known as investment funds are managed by professional management companies, and both is supervised by government regulators. In return for their investments, the investors receive units or shares from the management company there. It is an incredibly vast range of investment funds to choose from their investment goals and objectives must be described in the fund prospectus along with the assets.

- **Mutual Funds:** a mutual fund is a collection of stocks, bonds, cash and other securities that are managed by professionals. Generally people buy mutual funds because they want a simple way to invest in a diversified portfolio with the security of knowing that someone will be watching it. Here's an example of how a mutual fund works. Phill has been investing for a long time with consistently awesome returns and people are always asking him for investment tips and financial advice so Phill decides to start a fund where he will manage and invest for people. He registers with the authorities, gets the approval and sets up a mutual fund. He calls it "Phill Fund" because he is such an awesome investor and he is able to convince ten people to invest $1,000 in Phill fund. Each investor owns one chair of his mutual fund and each share is worth a thousand dollars. This is referred to as net average value with the cash Phill invest in some stocks and bonds and leaves a little leftover in cash. This portfolio is referred to as assets under management. Phill also takes a small percentage of the fund as his fee, this is called the asset under management fee.

- **Exchanged Traded Funds "ETF":** ETF is an index fund and a stock got married and started a family. Their children would be ETFs. ETFs have inherited traits from each parent just like index funds. Most ETFs are passively managed diversified and low-cost and just like stocks, ETFs are bought through a brokerage account and trade on an exchange at any time during the day. There are over 6,000 ETFs on 60 exchanges around the world with about 3 trillion dollars in assets. Here's how they work. Imagine ETFs are baskets and each basket holds actual securities, so for example a bonds basket could be packed with a collection of government or corporate bonds, the solar stocks basket holds real shares and companies that make solar panels. Now let's say you had $1000 and you wanted to buy gold. The problem is $1000 isn't going to buy a whole lot of gold, only about an ounce. It's really difficult not to mention risky to store your own gold, what would be a lot easier and safer is to invest your thousand dollars in a gold ETF. When you do that, you're not buying the gold itself, you're buying shares of a big basket of gold shares.

The trade just like stocks and those are the two big attractions of ETFs. You don't need to be wealthy to invest in them and they are simple to buy, sell and own.

- **Dividends**: a dividend is a cash distribution by a company to its shareholders. For example let's look at XX ice cream shop to open his first shop. XX gathers money from investors in issue shares. XX's ice cream is a hit and sales skyrocket, XX uses the company's profits to open up more and more shops. XX decides to focus on keeping sales strong at his existing shops and profits continue to roll in. XX now has the choice between investing his profits or simply paying them out to the shareholders. XX knows he can sell ice cream, he's not sure he can make a profit investing so he decides to pay out some of his profits directly to the shareholders. He holds back some profits in case of an emergency and pays out all the cash. This cash is a dividend, it can be increased or decreased yearly according to how XX's business performs.

### How to Analyze Stock

Investors depend on stock analysis to find potentially profitable stocks. Common ways to analyze stock include technical and fundamental analysis. Several components fall under fundamental analysis, including examination of a company's price-to-earnings ratio, earnings per share, book value and return on equity. Many investors also use the recommendations of financial analysts to analyze a stock. The type of stock analysis you implement is based on personal preference. Understand the different ways to analyze a stock to find the method that best fits your financial objectives.

### Learn the two basic types of stock analysis

When it comes to analyzing stocks, there are two basic ways you can go: fundamental analysis and technical analysis.

- Fundamental analysis is based on the assumption that a stock price doesn't necessarily reflect the true intrinsic value of the underlying business. Fundamental analysts use valuation metrics and other information to determine whether a stock is attractively priced. Fundamental analysis is designed for investors looking for excellent long-term returns.

- Technical analysis generally assumes that a stock's price reflects all available information and that prices generally move according to trends. In other words, by analyzing a stock's price history, you may be able to predict its future price behavior. If you've ever seen someone trying to identify patterns in stock charts or discussing moving averages, that's a form of technical analysis.

One important distinction is that fundamental analysis is intended to find long-term investment opportunities, while technical analysis typically focuses on short-term price fluctuations. We generally are advocates of fundamental analysis and believe that by focusing on great businesses trading at fair prices, investors can beat the market over time.

## Technical Analysis

Technical analysis studies the supply and demand of a stock within the market. Investors who use technical analysis believe that a stock's historical performance indicates how the stock will perform in the future. Little attention is given to the value of the company. Technical analysis places heavy focus on the study of trends, charts and patterns.

## P/E Ratio

A common method to analyzing a stock is studying its price-to-earnings ratio. You calculate the P/E ratio by dividing the stock's market value per share by its earnings per share. To determine the value of a stock, investors compare a stock's P/E ratio to those of its competitors and industry standards. Lower P/E ratios are seen as favorable by investors.

Companies report their profits to shareholders as earnings per share, or EPS for short. The price-to-earnings ratio, or P/E ratio, is a company's share price divided by its annual per-share earnings. For example, if a stock trades for $30.00 and the company's earnings were $2.00 per share over the past year, we'd say it traded for a P/E ratio of 15, or "15 times earnings." This is the most common valuation metric in fundamental analysis, and is useful for comparing companies in the same industry with similar growth prospects.

### Earnings Per Share

A company's earnings per share show how efficiently its revenue is flowing down to investors. An increasing EPS is taken as a good sign by investors. According to NASDAQ, the higher a company's EPS, the more your shares are worth, because investors seek to purchase a company's stock when earnings are high.

### PEG Ratio

The price-to-earnings growth ratio takes the P/E ratio a step further by considering the growth of a company. To calculate the PEG, you divide the P/E ratio by the 12-month growth rate. You estimate the future growth rate by looking at the company's historical growth rate. Investors typically consider a stock valuable if the PEG is lower than 1.

Different companies grow at different rates. The PEG ratio takes a stock's P/E ratio and divides by the expected annualized earnings growth rate over the next few years to level the playing field. For example, a stock with a P/E ratio of 20 and 10% expected earnings growth over the next five years would have a PEG ratio of 2. The idea is that a fast-growing company can be "cheaper" than a slower-growing one.

### Book Value

Another method used to analyze a stock is determining a company's price-to-book ratio. Investors typically use this method to find high-growth companies that are undervalued. The formula for P/B ratio equals the market price of a company's stock divided by its book value of equity. Book value of equity is derived by subtracting the book value of liabilities from the book value of assets. Investors view a low P/B ratio as a sign that the stock is potentially undervalued.

A company's book value is the net value of all of its assets. Think of book value as the amount of money a company would theoretically have if it shut down its business and sold everything it owned. The price-to-book or P/B ratio is a comparison of a company's stock price and its book value.

## Return on Equity

Investors use return on equity to determine how well a company produces positive returns for its shareholders. Analyzing ROE can help you find companies that are profit generators. ROE is calculated by dividing net income by average shareholders' equity. A continual increase in ROE is a good sign to investors.

## Analyst Recommendations

Many investors use analyst recommendations to quickly size up a stock. Analysts perform extensive fundamental and technical research, and they issue buy or sell recommendations. Before deciding to buy or sell shares, investors typically use analyst recommendations in conjunction with a stock analysis technique.

## How I look at a stock:

I personally look at the stock growth in the last 5 and 10 years. What was there average growth if it less then 11%. I will not invest into the company in my long-term portfolio. The 2nd thing that help me determine if a stock is worth trying to get if they are earning any money. Betting on a company with a bad financial situation is not where I want to be at. In my eye I need to they are making me money so that I can see the company around another 10-20 years. I compare all my stock to the average of the S&P 500. I also have 5% of my overall portfolio in more risky stock. These stocks are generally penny stocks that I believe in the core value of the company, but just haven't went mainstream.

My Portfolio is broken down into 25% growth stocks, 70% that are dividend investing stock, 5% into risky investment. Why do I have such a high focus on dividend paying stocks in my Investing account not my retirement account is that stocks are only price at what people are willing to pay for it. I want to have a passive income where they pay me to have the stock.

## Why invest in dividend stocks?

Whether you're looking to generate income or build long-term wealth for the future, buying stocks that pay dividends can be a wonderful investing strategy. This is because of the two-pronged nature of the way dividend investing rewards investors: recurring dividend payments and capital appreciation.

Let's look at an example. Say you buy 100 shares of a company for $10 each, and that company pays a $0.30 annual dividend. You would invest $1,000, and over the course of a year would receive $30 in dividend payments. That works out to a 3% yield -- not too shabby. What you choose to do with your dividends is up to you: You can reinvest them in shares of the company, buy stock in a different company, or buy some pizza and a yacht. Regardless of whether the company's stock price goes up or down, you receive those dividend payments if the company continues to make them.

## How Dividend Reinvestment Boosts Your Returns

Despite these trends, dividends remain a key element that can boost your overall investing returns. When you reinvest dividend payments to buy more shares of stock in your investments, you help your portfolio benefit from enhanced compounding effects. On a basic level, each dividend you reinvest entitles you to more dividend payments in the future, which can supercharge your investment returns. Say you invested in an S&P 500 index fund starting in January 2000 and held your investment until September 2020. Your average annualized return based on stock price gains alone would have been 4.2%, for a cumulative return of 136%. Pretty good, right? But if you'd reinvested all dividend payments back in the fund over the same period, your annualized return would have been 6.2%, for a cumulative return of 247%. Just reinvesting dividends would have nearly doubled your gains.

Play with the numbers a bit using this calculator and you can find even more dramatic effects. Say you invested

$10,000 in an S&P 500 index fund in January 1990. You'd have about $91,300 today based on price gains alone. But add in the dividend reinvestments, and you'd have nearly double that amount, or $180,000.

**Tax Benefits of Dividend Investing**

Dividend investing can provide valuable tax advantages for income investors. The Internal Revenue Service (IRS) doesn't treat all dividends as the same, however. There are two classes: "Qualified" dividends, taxed at the lower, long-term capital gains rate, and "unqualified" or "ordinary" dividends, which are taxed as regular income. Most dividends paid by U.S. corporations are qualified dividends. That means that if investors own the stock for 60 days (in most cases), the income from dividends is taxed at the long-term capital gains rate. Certain other dividends—from Real Estate Investment Trusts (REITs) or master limited partnerships (MLPs)— are typically classified as ordinary dividends and taxed as regular income. Money market funds and other cash-like instruments also pay ordinary dividends.

Dividends received in tax-advantaged retirement accounts, like individual retirement accounts (IRA) or 401(k)s, generally aren't subject to tax until you withdraw them.

**How to Evaluate Dividend Stocks**

Dividend yield is one tool for evaluating the best dividend-paying stocks. Many websites are devoted to helping investors find high-yielding dividend stocks, but just going with the highest dividend yield can be a bit deceiving. Let's say you're looking at a stock that paid $5 in annual dividends and had until recently been valued at $100 a share. But the company's business came under pressure, and its shares fell to $50—although it's still paying $5 in annual dividends. In a relatively short period of time, the dividend yield would've doubled to 10% from 5%. In this case, the rising dividend yield is a sign of stress, not a sign of a healthy company.

A company with a declining share price might be facing problems, and its board may need to reconsider the dividend. This highlights reliability as a key element for picking dividend-paying stocks. You need to ask yourself, "Is this company secure enough to keep paying the promised dividends—and perhaps even slowly increase them over time?" One place to find reliable dividend stocks is to look at stocks in the Dividend Aristocrats, a group of stocks that historically has increased dividend payments over time. Stocks in certain sectors, like real estate and utilities, may also pay higher dividends on average.

Another measure of good dividend stocks is the dividend payout ratio, which removes volatile stock prices from the equation by comparing a company's earnings to its dividend payment per share. If a company earns $2 per share in a given quarter and pays a dividend of $1 per share, its payout ratio is said to be 50%. Lower payout ratios should indicate more sustainable dividends—or a low payout ratio could mean that a company needs to increase its dividend. A payout ratio over 100% indicates a company is returning more money to shareholders than it is earning, and it may need to lower its dividend—or that its earnings are under pressure. A steadily rising payout ratio, on the other hand, could indicate that a company is healthy and generating reliable returns in a mature industry.

## How You Can Pursue Dividend Investing

If you'd like to start generating income with dividend investing, you might implement one of the following three strategies.

### Aim for High Dividend Yields

This is the classic strategy for dividend investing. The focus here would be on slow-growing, established companies with a lot of cash flow that pay high dividends. These kinds of investments make sense when you are looking to generate income right away. Just keep in mind that high yields aren't everything. The companies may not see as much growth in stock value as other companies with lower dividend yields.

### Choose High Dividend Growth

Investors with a longer time horizon can focus on buying stock in companies that are growing quickly but currently pay lower-than-average dividends. This won't yield as much income in the short term, but as a firm grows and its business matures, the dividend yield should rise gradually. Getting in early means investors can buy more shares and eventually earn more dividends. The cheaper "cost-on-yield" makes this a better long-term investment strategy.

## Pursue Dividend Capture

Dividend capture is a more active, hands-on approach to harvesting dividend income. With dividend capture, it's not necessary to hold shares of a company for a whole year or an entire quarter to earn the dividend. Instead, you swoop in and buy them right before the dividend is paid out. Then once you're paid, you sell them again so you're able to buy other stocks. But this isn't as easy as it sounds: To earn a quarterly or annual dividend payment, you must own a stock before the ex-dividend date, which is typically two weeks before the dividend is paid. Then, after the dividend is paid, you have to decide when to sell. This gets complicated and risky because share prices are volatile and may be lower once the dividend is paid than when you bought them.

Share price declines like this can easily wipe out the money you earned from the dividend—or more. And even if your shares increase in value, if you're not trading in a tax-advantaged retirement account, dividend capture can generate short-term capital gains that are taxed at the higher regular income rate.

### Risks of Dividend Investing

Every investing strategy involves risk, and dividend investing is no exception. The biggest risk is that dividends are never guaranteed. Companies can and do reduce and even eliminate their dividends. During the Covid-19 pandemic, some very prominent, old-guard stocks have done so: Wells Fargo, Dick's Sporting Goods, Carnival, Goodyear Tire & Rubber, HSBC, Airbus and Rolls Royce, to name a few. But there are more subtle risks. Diversification should always be top of mind for any investor, and someone who focuses too much on dividends is likely to ignore some sectors and classes of companies they need for good diversification. Young, fast-growing tech companies, for example, don't generally pay dividends.

Lack of diversification always exposes investors to increased volatility. Dividend-only investors can miss out on high-value growth in those sectors that might not be paying dividends or that pay uncompetitive dividends.

# Chapter Four

# How To Start Investing And Trading

"When it comes to investing, we want our money to grow with the highest rates of return, and the lowest risk possible. While there are no shortcuts to getting rich, there are smart ways to go about it." – Phil Town

Those who are starting to feel their mortality and old age may be considering investing in their future. There are many reasons why this is a great idea, with one being that social security analysts are claiming that it may not be available for those who are due to retire in twenty years.

Your greatest asset is YOU. Haven't you seen extremely gifted and talented people that you knew were not maximizing their potential? Rather than striving for the best, they were simply wasting precious time on lesser pursuits. Most people are either not aware of their true potential or decided to stop at a certain level and settle there, perhaps out of fear, complacency, or ignorance. Recognize that you are valuable to the world in some way--large or small. Invest the time and resources to shine forth your brilliance, so that your glow can warm others.

Now that you have a bit of a background about what stocks, shares and shareholders are, it is time to begin investing. Investing in stocks is exciting, but I must warn you. A lot of work goes into picking the right stock. A lot of work should go into it since you are putting your hard earned money into investing. It is similar to buying a house. Do you just make purchases based on what others are saying or do you do your due diligence. You check out the neighborhood, comps in the area, schools if you have kids, county statistics.

Here are the most important steps to take into consideration when you take a decision to start investing.

- **Learns the basics**

Personal finance and investing is an awesome thing to get into because you can dig as deep into it as you want or stay at the surface level. There is a reason why some of the smartest investing minds in the world (Warren Buffett) read for hours on end. The finance world evolves, markets change, and the way people behave with money moves around. With that being said, you need to learn the basics. What are the basics?

"Spend less than you make, invest the difference"

Spend – Create a budget. Fixed expenses and then fun money.

Make – Get a job that allows you to save a little bit of cash

Invest – Dollar Cost Average, 401k, Roth IRA, brokerage account, withdrawal rates.

It will be easy to go down a rabbit hole when reading about personal finance to the point where it might even intimidate you. Learn the basics and get started. There are plenty of free online resources that will help you understand best practices like which % of your budget towards certain items and how to invest. You have some time to iron out the details. The worst thing you can do is not start.

- **Keep it simple: Index Funds**

I don't know how else to say this but I would recommend you start off with index funds. I know it isn't what people is going to tell you but index funds will allow you to get a piece of the pie without the risk of individual stocks. The worst thing that could happen to you is you throw a grand in a stock based on a tip on Reddit and you get wiped out to the point where you don't even want to invest in the market anymore.

Understand that cycles happen. "Bulls make money, bears make money, pigs get slaughtered". Look into the top 10 companies by market cap for each decade. Companies come and go. I am not anti-stock at all. I recommend that people play around with stocks to avoid FOMO but only once they have enough in index funds to where compound interest takes over.

- **This isn't a get rich quick scheme**

Understand the game that you are playing. Investing Twitter and TV networks react to daily moves in the market. You aren't in it for the short term, you are in it for the long term. If you are in your early 20's you probably have a 30-40-year time horizon. Think of all the crazy world events that have happened in the last 30-40 years alone. COVID, 08 Financial Crisis, Iraq War, 9/11, Dot Com Crash, and then the 1987 Market Crash. All of those "world is ending" type events have led to a 9.42% average return before inflation. To tap into the power of compound interest you need to stay in the market for a long period of time.

- **Diversify and Reduce Risks**

Diversification is considered to be the only free lunch in investing. In a nutshell, by investing in a range of assets, you reduce the risk of one investment's performance severely hurting the return of your overall investment. You could think of it as financial jargon for "don't put all of your eggs in one basket."

In terms of diversification, the greatest amount of difficulty in doing this will come from investments in stocks. As mentioned earlier, the costs of investing in a large number of stocks could be detrimental to the portfolio. With a $1,000 deposit, it is nearly impossible to have a well-diversified portfolio, so be aware that you may need to invest in one or two companies (at the most) to begin with. This will increase your risk.

- **Brokerage Account**

In order to purchase a stock, you must go through a brokerage account or securities account which is what it is sometime referred to. A brokerage account is an investment account that allows you to buy and sell a variety of investments, such as stocks, bonds, mutual funds, and ETFs. Whether you're setting aside money for the future or saving up for a big purchase, you can use your funds whenever and however you want.

## Guidelines For Beginner Investors

### 1. Don't invest money you are going to need soon.

The stock market has its ups and downs — that is to be expected. Therefore, it's unrealistic to assume that you're going to earn huge profits in a short period of time. Start investing with the idea that you're putting your money away for five to 10 years. Don't invest money that you'll need to use for a down payment on a house in six months. Or, money you're supposed to use for rent in two months. It's too risky because if you sell your stock shares for less than you bought them, you'll lose money.

Instead, start investing with a small amount, and put money you'll need to access into your savings.

### 2. Don't purchase a stock just because someone else tells you to.

Do your own research about a company and decide for yourself if you want to invest in it. Your peer's talk about the company that's going to become "the next Facebook" may be tantalizing, but don't blindly follow their advice.

Here's what those people won't tell you: everyone has a different level of risk tolerance. Some people are more willing than others to take a short-term hit. One person's stock recommendation may be perfect for their portfolio, but too risky for yours. At the same time, be open-minded about learning from other peoples' experiences.

It's up to you to inform yourself about what you're putting your money into. When researching a company, read up on recent news about it and make sure you know who its customers are. A good rule of thumb is: don't buy a stock in a company if you can't explain what exactly that company does.

### 3. Think about how a company or service will impact society in the future.

The present is kind of like your context clues for the future. Pay attention to the industries people are talking about and the services that are impacting everyone's lives. Also, consider the areas society wants to improve in (sustainability, for example).

One of the best ways to stay informed is to read the news. You can also pick the brains of your friends and family members. Their expertise in a specific field could give you some valuable insight.

### 4. Make investing more fun by curating a portfolio that's reflective of your personal interests and values.

Channeling your passions through your portfolio is just a strategy for helping you feel less intimidated by investing. A good jumping off point is to invest in companies that align with your personal interests and values. If you're passionate about leading a healthy lifestyle, try looking into fitness companies, health brands, apparel brands, pharmaceutical companies, or health technology. Or perhaps you love home and interior design and want your portfolio to reflect that. Check out real estate firms, home goods brands, and architecture companies.

Diversification is a safe approach to make sure you don't put all your eggs in one basket (i.e. only investing in travel brands or only investing in energy companies). So, do some research into how the things you're passionate about have been making waves in different sectors.

**5. Buy and hold your stocks for a long time to give them a chance to grow.**

Too many investing newbies get caught up in the tiny worries — the small potatoes — when it comes to buying stocks. They check their portfolio 20 times a day to see if their shares are on the rise yet. They freak out when the stock they just bought drops by a few cents. They consider selling as soon as the stock makes a couple of bucks.

Yes, there have been some bumps along the road but that's to be expected. Besides, just look at how industries roared back to life in the decade after 2008! The market is very emotionally driven and has its high points and low points. But over time, the market generally trends upward. This is why holding your investments long-term is a fruitful strategy.

Whether you buy just two shares of an impactful company at $100 or $101, you'll still likely see gains in 5, 10, and 15 years and beyond.

**6. Think of investing as a way of saving for the future rather than as spending money for right now.**

This is a psychological trick that I use on myself whenever I feel like not adding money to the stock market for a month or two and instead bulking up a lower-return savings account. Even though the money is leaving my account to "buy" a share of a company, I look at it as adding to the nest egg that I'm building up. A simple change in the way I word an action is enough to trigger a different type of understanding. It also helps to budget a specified amount to put toward stocks each month.

### 7. Don't FOMO

Yes we all heard it. You know that feeling when people are posting crazy gains on these new stocks. It's so so easy to get sucked in to thinking, if I just put in some money right now I can get 10-20-50% gains in a few days! It's already up 200% this month, surely it will keep going!?

This takes some real patience to keep your head cool and realize it could very well be overbought and the downside risk is just a lot higher than potential. I've seen several sector hypes. We all remember the crypto bubble, the weed bubble and now lately the EV bubble. They all come and go and the more of these you been in from the start the easier it is to realize what's going on.

## 8. If the company keeps growing, why sell?

Taking profit is good however not always the best thing to do. If the stock you have keeps growing and keeps crushing earnings. Why should you sell? Why just not keep it for years, it sure can be tempting but are you sure that money could be spent better elsewhere when it's easily growing in your winning stock.

## 9. Never regret that you didn't buy more

We all been here. Why the hell didn't I buy more of Amazon? Why didn't I just put my whole paycheck in this stock!?

You can never do this. It won't lead to anything, you can't fix it and you honestly did the best decisions at the time with the information you had. Realize that at the time this was the best decision, of course hindsight it looks like you could have done a better decision.

## Mistakes To Avoid

Getting into trading is no easy task. Every trader will need to find his own path to success and profitability. Whether we are talking about the instruments you will choose, the strategies you will apply, or the indicators you will follow, for many people they will all be different combinations of things. And those will depend on your interests, influences, how your mind works, and many other things. Some will trade the news, others will trade only according to certain technical indicators of their choice. And that is all okay, as long as you are learning, and in the end, making a profit. However, as different as these paths to success can be, there are quite a few common rules to follow and mistakes to avoid. In this article, we will be looking at the most common mistakes traders make. These mistakes are especially common to beginner traders, however, some are also prevalent in the more experienced of minds. These mistakes range from poor decision making to lack of preparation, to trading based on emotion. And they are what usually breaks a trader. A lot of them are interrelated and you will easily get the full picture as we go along.

So, without further ado, let's dive into the most common mistakes that traders make, which you should avoid.

## 1. Lack of preparation

One of, if not the most important mistakes traders make is trading without enough preparation. This is especially true for beginner traders since they are the ones at most risk here. Think of not being experienced enough to trade, not knowing how to trade the markets in the first place, but instead of going with a demo trading account, or going small, you open an account with a broker and make a big deposit. This might sound far fetched for some, but it does happen. Another day or week passes, and the account gets burned. If you are looking to spend money gambling – go for it, but know what you are going for and know what you can expect to get from trading at high stakes without knowing what you are doing. Which is exactly that – a quickly burnt account.

This common mistake can also apply to experienced traders. Think about knowing what you are doing for the most part, however, not doing your homework. Every trade needs to be disciplined, thought about and not impulsive. If you are trading weekly oil inventories, on the basis of statistical analysis, and you do not crunch the numbers, but rather just go for it expecting to wing it from your experience, it is still the same mistake you are making. That is, you are not prepared for that particular trade, and you should not be going into it. Always try to stay disciplined and conscious of your decision making. It is rather easy to let yourself get loose and start gambling with your money. It is much harder, however, to recover those bad losses that you could have avoided in the first place.

## 2. Expecting to get rich quick

Another common mistake you can make prior to even starting to trade is expecting to get rich fast. If you do have this expectation somewhere deep in your mind, you have to realize, you will need to let it go. This powerful expectation will be fuel to your fear and emotion-based trading. It will affect most aspects of your trading, especially your decision making. Why so? Because you will be going through an amplified emotional rollercoaster that will mess you up at least whenever things go wrong. Think of making a losing trade, and fearing to realize the losses, only to dig your hole deeper. Or think of realizing those losses, but feeling like things are not going your way the way they are supposed to be going. And then making an emotionally-charged trade to make up for your losses that day. Eventually, this pattern will lead you to make bad decisions, and blow up your account or keep losing money.

Most experienced and successful traders know that they can expect to be profitable in the long term, however, it is a long term. They are less affected by both, the gains and the losses. They are much more neutral and know they will be making losses at times, which is part of the life of a trader. This does not affect how they feel about a particular trade or their strategy as a whole. They keep disciplined and focused, and do not let false expectations get the best of them.

### 3. Not treating trading like a business

Many people that are attracted to trading usually like to be their own bosses. They generally don't like to be told what to do by a superior. While it can be a good trait, inspiring you to create your own business, it does come with its own challenges. For instance, if you are of such a personality, you might be too loose on yourself. However, if you are going into trading, if the only boss you ever have is you, you better make sure that that boss is the strictest boss you will ever have. That is, treat your trading like it is a business and really, be your own boss, in its fullest sense.

That might mean you will have to narrow down your focus and cut loose other activities you have taken up or enjoy doing in your spare time. That may mean that you will have to take trading full time. Or at least see it as a full-time activity in your future. While there are exceptions – for instance, having to work another job to build up that capital for your trading account, generally you are looking to treat it as a full-time business in the long run. If you don't, you have a high risk of not staying on top of things, not being prepared enough, etc. and etc.

## 4. Entering a trade without a plan

Every trade not only has to have a reason behind it. It also has to have a plan. That is, what are you going to do if the price goes in your favor? What are you going to do if the price goes against you? Which take profit and stop loss levels will you set? What if the price goes sideways? What will you do if an unexpected event comes about? These are only some of the questions you need to be asking yourself whenever entering a trade. If you enter a trade without such a plan, you will set yourself up for a big potential disaster.

Imagine not knowing what to do in each scenario, and one of those scenarios plays out. You will be playing a guessing game at best. This is where preparation that we have talked about before comes about. You will need to prepare yourself for every scenario there is, broadly speaking, to avoid making bad decisions.

## 5. Allocating too much capital to a single trade

Trading involves losses. For some strategies, the nature of them can be such that more than 50% of your trades will incur losses. (However, you will make up for them by having larger wins than losses.) Not only do you need to be mentally prepared for that, but you also have to play it smart with your money. Capital management is key here, and you do not ever want to be allocating too much capital to a single trade. That is because you do not know which trades will perform well, and which ones will not. You do not know which ones will be profitable, and which ones will incur a loss.

It may sometimes seem like you know exactly which direction the trade is going this time. Like it is the trade of the month, and you need to invest heavily in this trade. However, bear in mind that this is mostly your fear of missing out playing games with you here. In reality, and in general, you have roughly equal chances of making a profit today versus tomorrow. So, do not allocate too much capital to a single trade.

## 6. Trading without a stop loss

Another big mistake is actually having no stop losses in your positions. It is a common mistake made by those just beginning to trade. It might seem risky to put a stop loss on your position – what if the price rebounds just after it hits the stop loss? However, an even larger mistake is to not have any stop loss in the first place. You should know what price level change means that your trade did not go as planned. That would mean that your call was wrong on this trade, and you need to get out of it. Making and realizing losses is okay, and is a normal part of trading. No one successful trader can make profitable after profitable trade without ever incurring a loss. You should always keep that in mind and be sure to have stop losses in your strategy.

## 7. If you keep losing, do not keep trading

This common mistake mostly comes about due to two things. First, you might be having a really bad day, where nothing is going your way. Second, your strategy might simply not be working in the long run, and that's why you keep losing. As far as the first one goes, if you are having a bad day where nothing is going your way, it is usually best to call it a day and just defer trading to another day. If you don't, you are at risk of making bad decisions due to being stressed out and emotions coming into play. Trading is a stressful occupation and persistent or large losses can break even the toughest and most experienced of traders. Do not keep putting yourself down for having a bad day, it happens to everyone.

As far as the second one goes, sometimes your strategy simply does not work. Whether it is due to bad timing of the market, or some inherent flaws in the strategy, if you keep losing on your strategy in the long run, do not keep trading – try and make adjustments to your strategy, or simply look for a better one. It is probably one of the harder things to do, since it may feel like a defeat, however, bear in mind you may have to lose a few battles to win the war.

## 8. Trying to predict the news

News trading may seem lucrative because there is so much action going on at the time. More action means volatility, which means more potential and quicker gains. Who wouldn't want to make 50 pips in a few seconds? However, there is no free lunch in trading, and volatility has a downside too: whatever applies to the upside, also applies to the downside. That is, you are equally likely to lose or make a profit if you are trying to predict the unpredictable.

While it is sometimes possible to somewhat gauge what is the more likely outcome based on statistical analysis, it is usually extremely hard to predict news releases, such as the Non-Farm Payrolls, for example. Especially if you are a beginner, and are there just for the action and for the excitement, it is best to steer clear of entering a position before the news release comes out.

## 9. Trading assets with little volume

This especially applies to low volume stocks. You do not want to be trading low volume assets or during periods when there is low volume. This can sometimes be before crucial news releases, such as Non-Farm Payrolls or company quarterly releases, or trading hours in other sessions. Trading against this will result in you having to chase a wide spread and take on a much worse price than you need to.

In this chapter, we have outlined 9 of the most common mistakes made by both beginners and more experienced traders. They ranged from preparation to decision making, to capital management and more. What probably is beginning to become obvious is that trading involves a lot of discipline. Since it is easy to lose yourself in emotion and impulsiveness, it is a very useful trait in trading. Also, preparation and knowing what you are doing is key, as it will allow you to avoid some big errors and save you losses.

It is said, it's always best to learn from others' mistakes, rather than your own ones. However, it is usually a very hard thing to do. Hopefully, this article will help you avoid some of them, and not keep doing the same ones over and over again, by being more conscious of them.

## Wealthy People Sources of Income

## 7 Income Streams of Millionaires [According To The IRS]

We have all had worked a 9-5 job where it seemed like you'll never be able to get ahead. It's difficult, if not impossible, to build real wealth when you're working a minimum wage or low-income job for someone else and helping them create wealth.

So how do millionaires earn income? Millionaires have essential 7 income streams, some passive, that allow them to earn money all the time. They don't trade time for money like at most jobs. Instead, they're creators and innovative businesspeople.

I've read through this document by the IRS, which shows the biggest differences in the tax returns of millionaire's vs regular people. Below, I'll go into detail covering all 7 of the income streams millionaires and the wealthy use and give your ideas for implementing them yourself. In this book we will only discuss on how to create your wealth with dividend income and capital gain off stocks.

## 1. Earned Income

Earned income is one of the first income streams of millionaires and is one that most people understand. Earned income comes directly from your job.

Most people rely solely on earned income for their livelihood and that's a HUGE mistake. You're trading hours of your life for dollars. When you need more money, you work more hours. The problem is that everyone gets the same 24 hours in a day and there's only so much work you can do.

So how this would work is if you have a job but want to earn more income, you can either try to get a job that pays you more per hour or take on a second or third job. This may mean working overnights or on weekends. The problem with this is that you're continuing to trade more and more of your time for money. Instead, your goal should be trading your time for more money.

### How To Increase Your Earned Income?

If you want to increase your earned income like the rich do the best way to do so is to increase your knowledge in your field or to start getting more certification to help you become more valuable. One example of this is to increase your skills and knowledge.

If you're stuck working a minimum wage job, what skills would you need in order to become a manager or assistant manager? Look for free business training or find a business mentor who can show you the ropes.

Something as simple as going from a store employee to a manager can increase your hourly wage by $10 or more. You're still working the same number of hours but are getting paid significantly more per hour.

### How To Increase Income But Work Less?

Everyone has the same 24 hours in a day. If you want to get out of the thought process of trading your life hours for money, then you'll want to cultivate a specialty skill.

Specialists in a field are some of the most highly paid people. They can earn hundreds of dollars an hour which allows them to work a lot less. You may be surprised to know that you don't have to have a PhD or be a world-known specialist for this to be the case. The internet has opened up a huge number of online careers that once weren't available. They're completely remote and fancy schooling isn't required. Your experience and results are what matter.

One example of this is becoming online bookkeeper. It was once a field where a degree is not needed, and you were hired as a full-time company employee. Now, you can easily start your own freelance bookkeeping management business without a degree. Specialists who get results can earn $200 or more per hour. If you're looking for more ideas, check out these stays at home jobs.

## 2. Dividend Income

Dividend income is a form of income that's paid from the shares of a company you own. Another common name for these is dividend stocks. This is a passive form of income since you don't have to actively buy or sell stocks. You're considered a shareholder in the company you own the dividend stock in. At the end of the year, if you owned 1000 shares of dividend stock and each earned $2 in dividend income, that's $2000. As you scale this up with more and more shares, the earnings are significant.

The key is to pick the right dividend stock which is easier said than done. You also risk the company going out of business and your shares becoming worthless. Most dividend stocks have an extremely low yield of 2-3% so if you're young, investing in well-diversified index funds may be a better option since the growth potential is higher. You can also find High yield dividend is 10-5%, but generally those are really high risk and will required you to take some time and research to find what best fit you.  As with any investment, make sure you have a complete understanding before investing and consult a licensed financial professional.

### 3. Rental Income

Rental income is the money that you earn from renting out anything someone is willing to rent. I had rented out power tools to coworker while I was a diesel mechanic, he couldn't afford to buy quality power tools out right. He was willing to pay me 150 dollar a month to rent few of my extra power tools that I had laying around.  I had paid total of 500 dollar for the tools he was renting from me and he borrow the power tools for 8 months. I had made $1200 from allowing him to rent out the power tools and after the purchase of the power tools of 900 dollar and used them for 2 years.

More commonly this could include single-family homes or apartment buildings renting to everyday people to live in, or it could be commercial real estate renting property to other businesses to use.

Most millionaires own a large amount of real estate because it's such a powerful type of income stream.

Land is a finite resource; once it's all bought, more isn't going to be created. The wealthy understand this and buy real estate in popular locations or up and coming neighborhoods because those assets appreciate faster.

One of the biggest drawbacks of real estate is the large amount of money required upfront. Even if you get a loan, you'll still need to put down a sizable deposit to the bank. Real estate's greatest weakness is also its greatest strength. With real estate, if you want to buy a $200,000 house, a bank will often loan you the money with only a 10% down payment of $20,000. If you wanted to buy $200,000 worth of stocks, you'd need $200,000 on hand. No bank is going to loan you money to buy stocks because they deem the risk too high.

Real estate is considered a much less risky investment by banks because there's a tangible item and the housing market is generally less volatile. It's not less risky for the home buyer because if you can't find tenants or come on hard times, your mortgage still needs to be paid or the bank will take your house.

People who over-leverage their investment property purchases have a high net worth built on a house of cards. It takes only one economic downturn or issues with one of the properties for it all to come crashing down. That's why when going the real estate route, it's important to not bite off more than you can financially handle.

## Why Will Banks Loan You Money For Real Estate But Not Stocks?

Banks will lend people money for real estate but not stocks because real estate is considered a lower risk. Property owners have insurance on their homes which is something you can't get with stocks.

Banks see real estate as more secure than stocks because there's the value of the land as well as the value of the home that they can force a sale for if they need to recuperate their costs.

With stocks, the price you buy them for is the price they're worth. This isn't the case with real estate. Sometimes, life events happen where someone is desperate to sell a property. If you're savvy at identifying investment real estate, you can purchase a property for less than it's worth.

## 4. Royalties & Licensing

Royalties are a powerful passive income stream for someone who creates their own products. It can be a process or idea that you then license the rights for others to use for a fee. Someone's ideas and created products are considered privately owned so you aren't allowed to take them without their consent. It's considered theft.

The largest example of this is for book authors. A book author licenses their work to the publishing house. The publisher then formats, prints, and sells the book. Depending on the book deal the author negotiated, they get a percentage of the profits called royalties.

While it may take a year or more for the author to write the book, they can continue to earn royalties for years after publication. This is a wonderfully lucrative passive income stream if you have lots of ideas and can produce products or get patents. Being an innovator and creator is one of the main habit differences between a rich vs poor person. People who create wealth don't waste their time being unoriginal.

## 5. Interest

Interest income is the money you earn from lending your personal money to someone else. You can earn interest from a bank, money market account, lending it to the government, Certificates of Deposit, and many other ways. Earning money in the form of interest is exactly like the money that credit card companies charge or the interest you pay on your mortgage. You earn a small percentage on the money you put for others to temporarily borrow. Earning interest from your bank has no risk because they're FDIC insured. If the bank makes a bad investment and loses your money, you'll get it back because the federal government insures it.

You can also earn interest if you sell a business and allow the buyer to pay you back in installments over time plus interest. When doing this, you won't have all the money from the business you sold immediately but if you deem the buyer a low risk, you may decide this type of situation is ideal.

For example, you could sell your business or a franchise and allow the buyer to take 5 years to pay the full amount to you. Every month, the buyer would pay you the set principle amount plus the percentage interest you settled on. During this time, the buyer is running the company but if they default on the loan, you'd be able to take the business back. Of course, this would all depend on the contract you set up with your lawyers.

## 6. Capital Gains

Capital gains are the money you get due to the increase in value of an asset you're selling. It's the positive difference between the sale price of the asset and the original purchase price. This includes stocks, real estate property, bonds, jewelry, coin collections, or cars.

Capital gains differs from investment income though. Capital gains are purely the profits from selling an investment for more than its worth. Investment income is a term that includes capital gains, dividends, interest, and other profits made.

To earn money through capital gains, most common ways are buying properties at a low price and selling them for profit or buying growth stock funds and selling them once they've increased in value.

Capital gains does have a tax implication so make sure to check with your tax professional before selling off large assets.

## 7. Business Profits

Business profits are different than salaries. Salaries are the amount you earn for doing your job. It can be hourly or an agreed upon yearly sum. Business profits is the money left over in the business after all other expenses have been paid. Business profit can be made through advertising, selling products, or providing services. All money that a business earns gets added into the business' profit tally for the year.

Some business owners reinvest this excess money back into the business but they can also take it as a bonus. Often, business owners will wait until after taxes to take a lump sum business profit. This is hard-earned money for creating a successful business. Since business profit may be inconsistent, instead of increasing one's salary and potentially hurting the business, keeping the same salary and giving oneself a bonus of extra profit is a more conservative option.

## How Many Income Streams Do You Have?

Now that you know the 7 income streams of millionaires, compare that with how many you currently have. Most people only have one or two with a job and rental property being the most common.

The benefits of having multiple income streams in that you're more recession proof. Financial hiccups are less likely to derail your trajectory. If you lost your job or a tenant can't pay rent, you aren't left bankrupt. This can create an immense peace of mind. By leveraging your time now to create additional income streams, you can be on the path to ensure your family's financial security. During the time of the pandemic I wasn't worry about losing my job. I personally have 5 stream of income and working on trying to get all 7 streams of income, so that I can live a stress free life if I lose 1 or 2 of my stream of income. Right now, they all together bring a great deal of wealth, but losing 1 would financial strain how I live and will have to slow down on my investing dramatically.

Wealthy people understand that there's only so much money to be earned by trading your time for money. If you truly want to build wealth, then passive income streams are where your time should be spent. There's no truly passive income stream where you never have to put in effort to earn money. Most passive income avenues require intense work upfront but allow the ability to earn for years without any additional effort.

In the next chapter this book will go over in more detailed on what a stock is and focus on learning the basic information of what each stock is. This will help with the other chapter when discussing on methods and example on creating a million dollar.

## How to go from 0 to 1 million

Investing isn't as scary as it sounds. While all investments carry risk, not all of them are equally risky. Before hitting the stock market with a tax-advantaged account, you can invest without taking too much risk and in places that might earn you more reward.

Most retirement and related accounts invest in the stock market, but through a combination of stocks, bonds, CDs, mutual funds and other types of investments. The benefit of investing through these types of accounts is that they're tax-free (or tax-deferred), leaving more money in your pocket. Before you play the market through a standard brokerage account, here are the investment accounts you should max out.

Let look at the first way you can become a millionaire by using a target day index fund. What is a target date? Target-date funds are a variety of actively managed fund that are designed to "mature" at a specific time. Passively managed index funds simply buy and hold a basket of securities that also fit the fund's objective without any portfolio turnover.

For this example in this section, we are going to used the following information through out all of the example:

- Amount Invested a month: 500

- Goal: 1 Million USD

- Show 30 year return

- All fund will be place in a ROTH IRA

Target Date fund: Is an investment fund that automatically changes the closer you are to retirement.  Here are some real examples of target date fund options (as of 2020). Notice how the funds with a closer target date are invested less in stocks and more in bonds:

- 2065 Fund: 90% in stocks; 10% in bonds

- 2040 Fund: 85% in stocks; 15% in bonds

- 2020 Fund: 55% in stocks; 45% in bonds

When the funds start in 2020 the return for annual will be 11% and toward last 15 year the average return will be 8%

I will break it down into 2 section for a target date:

# Section 1 first 15 year: 11% return

| Results Summary | |
| --- | --- |
| Starting amount | $0.00 |
| Years | 15 years |
| Additional contributions | $500.00 per month |
| Rate of return | 11% compounded annually |
| Total amount you will have contributed | $90,000.00 |
| Total interest | $128,536.08 |
| Total at end of investment | $218,536.08 |

Savings Balance

| Year | Additions | Interest | Balance |
| --- | --- | --- | --- |
| Start | $0.00 | | $0.00 |
| 1 | $6,000.00 | $351.80 | $6,351.80 |
| 2 | $6,000.00 | $1,050.53 | $13,402.33 |
| 3 | $6,000.00 | $1,826.06 | $21,228.39 |
| 4 | $6,000.00 | $2,686.93 | $29,915.32 |
| 5 | $6,000.00 | $3,642.47 | $39,557.79 |
| 6 | $6,000.00 | $4,703.14 | $50,260.93 |
| 7 | $6,000.00 | $5,880.51 | $62,141.44 |
| 8 | $6,000.00 | $7,187.37 | $75,328.81 |
| 9 | $6,000.00 | $8,637.96 | $89,966.77 |
| 10 | $6,000.00 | $10,248.14 | $106,214.91 |
| 11 | $6,000.00 | $12,035.45 | $124,250.36 |
| 12 | $6,000.00 | $14,019.33 | $144,269.69 |
| 13 | $6,000.00 | $16,221.47 | $166,491.16 |
| 14 | $6,000.00 | $18,665.83 | $191,156.99 |
| 15 | $6,000.00 | $21,379.09 | $218,536.08 |

## Section last 15 years: 8% return

| Results Summary | |
|---|---|
| Starting amount | $218,536.00 |
| Years | 15 years |
| Additional contributions | $500.00 per month |
| Rate of return | 8% compounded annually |
| Total amount you will have contributed | $308,536.00 |
| Total interest | $554,586.25 |
| Total at end of investment | $863,122.25 |

Savings Balance

| Year | Additions | Interest | Balance |
|---|---|---|---|
| Start | $218,536.00 | | $218,536.00 |
| 1 | $6,000.00 | $17,739.81 | $242,275.81 |
| 2 | $6,000.00 | $19,639.01 | $267,914.82 |
| 3 | $6,000.00 | $21,690.12 | $295,604.94 |
| 4 | $6,000.00 | $23,905.33 | $325,510.27 |
| 5 | $6,000.00 | $26,297.75 | $357,808.02 |
| 6 | $6,000.00 | $28,881.57 | $392,689.59 |
| 7 | $6,000.00 | $31,672.09 | $430,361.68 |
| 8 | $6,000.00 | $34,685.90 | $471,047.58 |
| 9 | $6,000.00 | $37,940.74 | $514,988.32 |
| 10 | $6,000.00 | $41,456.02 | $562,444.34 |
| 11 | $6,000.00 | $45,252.48 | $613,696.82 |
| 12 | $6,000.00 | $49,352.69 | $669,049.51 |
| 13 | $6,000.00 | $53,780.92 | $728,830.43 |
| 14 | $6,000.00 | $58,563.37 | $793,393.80 |
| 15 | $6,000.00 | $63,728.45 | $863,122.25 |

As you can see investing in a target date will not make you a millionaire in 30 years set in the example, but it can make you a millionaire from this investing by waiting 2 more year and continue your investing.

| Results Summary | |
|---|---|
| Starting amount | $218,536.00 |
| Years | 17 years. |
| Additional contributions | $500.00 per month |
| Rate of return | 8% compounded annually |
| Total amount you will have contributed | $320,536.00 |
| Total interest | $699,224.23 |
| Total at end of investment | $1,019,760.23 |

Savings Balance

| Year | Additions | Interest | Balance |
|---|---|---|---|
| Start | $218,536.00 | | $218,536.00 |
| 1 | $6,000.00 | $17,739.81 | $242,275.81 |
| 2 | $6,000.00 | $19,639.01 | $267,914.82 |
| 3 | $6,000.00 | $21,690.12 | $295,604.94 |
| 4 | $6,000.00 | $23,905.33 | $325,510.27 |
| 5 | $6,000.00 | $26,297.75 | $357,808.02 |
| 6 | $6,000.00 | $28,881.57 | $392,689.59 |
| 7 | $6,000.00 | $31,672.09 | $430,361.68 |
| 8 | $6,000.00 | $34,685.90 | $471,047.58 |
| 9 | $6,000.00 | $37,940.74 | $514,988.32 |
| 10 | $6,000.00 | $41,456.02 | $562,444.34 |
| 11 | $6,000.00 | $45,252.48 | $613,696.82 |
| 12 | $6,000.00 | $49,352.69 | $669,049.51 |
| 13 | $6,000.00 | $53,780.92 | $728,830.43 |
| 14 | $6,000.00 | $58,563.37 | $793,393.80 |
| 15 | $6,000.00 | $63,728.45 | $863,122.25 |
| 16 | $6,000.00 | $69,306.73 | $938,428.98 |
| 17 | $6,000.00 | $75,331.25 | $1,019,760.23 |

We can away change the number on how much we can invest each month, but for standard all these examples we will keep it at $500. In this example it shows that you can become a millionaire in 32 years investing in a target day fund. Using national average found off fidelity and Vanguard.

Key thing to note is that we did not include the fees in these example or employee match, But I used this example for the used if we put this in a Roth IRA which in 2020 the limit you can put in is $6,000 a year.

The next example we are going to use the SP 500 average return in the last 10 year as of 2020. S&P 500 has done slightly better than the historic 10-year average, with an annual average return of 13.6% in the past 10 years.

| Results Summary | |
|---|---|
| Starting amount | $0.00 |
| Years | 30 years |
| Additional contributions | $500.00 per month |
| Rate of return | 13.6% compounded annually |
| Total amount you will have contributed | $180,000.00 |
| Total interest | $1,941,654.84 |
| Total at end of investment | $2,121,654.84 |

Savings Balance

| Year | Additions | Interest | Balance |
|------|-----------|----------|---------|
| Start | $0.00 | | $0.00 |
| 1 | $6,000.00 | $433.40 | $6,433.40 |
| 2 | $6,000.00 | $1,308.33 | $13,741.73 |
| 3 | $6,000.00 | $2,302.27 | $22,044.00 |
| 4 | $6,000.00 | $3,431.38 | $31,475.38 |
| 5 | $6,000.00 | $4,714.07 | $42,189.45 |
| 6 | $6,000.00 | $6,171.16 | $54,360.61 |
| 7 | $6,000.00 | $7,826.44 | $68,187.05 |
| 8 | $6,000.00 | $9,706.85 | $83,893.90 |
| 9 | $6,000.00 | $11,842.97 | $101,736.87 |
| 10 | $6,000.00 | $14,269.60 | $122,006.47 |
| 11 | $6,000.00 | $17,026.27 | $145,032.74 |
| 12 | $6,000.00 | $20,157.85 | $171,190.59 |
| 13 | $6,000.00 | $23,715.33 | $200,905.92 |
| 14 | $6,000.00 | $27,756.60 | $234,662.52 |
| 15 | $6,000.00 | $32,347.51 | $273,010.03 |
| 16 | $6,000.00 | $37,562.73 | $316,572.76 |
| 17 | $6,000.00 | $43,487.28 | $366,060.04 |
| 18 | $6,000.00 | $50,217.57 | $422,277.61 |
| 19 | $6,000.00 | $57,863.15 | $486,140.76 |
| 20 | $6,000.00 | $66,548.53 | $558,689.29 |
| 21 | $6,000.00 | $76,415.13 | $641,104.42 |
| 22 | $6,000.00 | $87,623.58 | $734,728.00 |
| 23 | $6,000.00 | $100,356.42 | $841,084.42 |
| 24 | $6,000.00 | $114,820.88 | $961,905.30 |
| 25 | $6,000.00 | $131,252.51 | $1,099,157.81 |
| 26 | $6,000.00 | $149,918.84 | $1,255,076.65 |
| 27 | $6,000.00 | $171,123.80 | $1,432,200.45 |
| 28 | $6,000.00 | $195,212.66 | $1,633,413.11 |
| 29 | $6,000.00 | $222,577.58 | $1,861,990.69 |
| 30 | $6,000.00 | $253,664.15 | $2,121,654.84 |

As you can see if you invest into S&P 500 for 30 years you will hit the millionaire mark at 25 years. That is 7 year earlier than the Average target date fund.  This would be great in 30 years if you had it in a ROTH IRA this is all tax free. Also, you only invested a total of $180,000 and due to compound interested you end up with $2.1 million.

The next example we are going to take a riskier approach and invest into ARKK. There 5-year return rate as of 6/30/2020 is 29.09%. The Ark Innovation (ARKK) ETF is a fund created and managed by Ark Invest CEO Cathie Wood. Ark Invest is a futurist fund that manages billions of dollars in assets with the goal of investing in the technologies and innovators that will shape our future. These technologies include robotics & AI, genomics, the future of the internet and fintech, each with their own specific ETF assigned to specialize in those topics, with the Ark Innovation fund built on the best investments from each fund.

This is a very risky up and coming ETF and don't recommend this to someone who is close to retirement. This show that you will become a millionaire by the 18 year of investing. That is 7 years earlier then if you invested in the SP 500. Young people are confident about their financial futures. A recent survey from TD Ameritrade found that 53 percent of millennials expect to become millionaires at some point in their lives, if they aren't already.

While 23 percent believe they'll hit $1 million by age 50 or older, many expect to get there more quickly.

A full 19 percent say they'll become a millionaire by age 40 and 7 percent predict it'll happen by 30. But what if you want to speed up the process and reach that milestone in the next 15 years? It could be possible, if you're willing to work for it — and put away much more each month than the average American.

Using Bankrate's millionaire calculator. Here's how much you'll need to put away, depending on the amount you already have invested.

To become a millionaire in 15 years with no savings:

- With a 4 percent rate of return: $4,075 per month

- With a 6 percent rate of return: $3,500 per month

- With an 8 percent rate of return: $2,945 per month

- With a 10 percent rate of return $2,500 per month

- With a 12 percent rate of return $2,120 per month

To become a millionaire in 15 years with $10,000 in savings:

- With a 4 percent rate of return: $4,000 per month

- With a 6 percent rate of return: $3,375 per month

- With an 8 percent rate of return: $2,850 per month

- With a 10 percent rate of return $2,400 per month

- With a 12 percent rate of return $2,000 per month

To become a millionaire in 15 years with $20,000 in savings:

- With a 4 percent rate of return: $3,930 per month

- With a 6 percent rate of return: $3,325 per month

- With an 8 percent rate of return: $2,775 per month

- With a 10 percent rate of return $2,300 per month

- With a 12 percent rate of return $1,890 per month

But it's important to keep in mind that these calculations don't account for the many variables that can affect wealth over several decades, including windfalls, emergencies and rises or dips in the market. Of course, saving hundreds or thousands a month is an ambitious goal. Even $1,000 a month is more than most Americans can manage. But getting into the habit of saving any amount will be great for you in the long run.

Here are a few simple, low-stress ways to start investing:

- Sign up for your employer's 401(k) plan and take full advantage of any company match, which essentially gives you free money

- Contribute to a Roth IRA or traditional IRA, an individual retirement account that offers tax breaks

- Use micro-investing apps such as Acorns, which help you begin by investing small amounts of what it calls your "spare change."

The app rounds up your purchases to the nearest dollar and automatically puts your coins to work

- Try other apps that aim to make investing simple

- Consider automated investing services known as robo-advisors that can help you out no matter how much you have in the bank

- Research low-cost index funds, which Warren Buffett recommends

## Successful Investing Stories

### Jesse Lauriston Livermore

Jesse Livermore was an American stock investor known for trading his personal account to over $100 million during the 1929 Great Depression — a feat which earned him the nickname, the Great Bear of Wall Street. He was born in 1877 in Shrewsbury, Massachusetts to a very poor family. The family would later move to Acton when he was still a kid to start a farming business.

But Jesse never liked the idea of farming, and with his mother's blessings, he ran away to Boston. He first became involved with stocks when he was only 14 years old. Then, he was working at the Paine Webber brokerage firm in Boston posting stock quotes. He would make price projections and note them, and later, he would check how accurate his projections were.

Convinced of his accuracy, in 1892 (when he was only 15) he started putting his price projections into use by making bets at a bucket shop. In a short time, he was making more money from his bets than he earned from Paine Webber. He quit his job and continued betting. In no time, he has made enough money to move to Wall Street and start his investing career in earnest.

It took him time to find his feet in New York City, but he eventually did. His first big profit came in 1901 when he bought the shares of Northern Pacific and made over 400% in profit, effectively raising his worth from about $10,000 to more than $50,000. He was highly skilled at identifying stocks that would make great moves and was never afraid to go short on stocks he thought would fall. He would start with a small order to see if he was right and build up his position later.

But the authorities sometimes stopped some of his moves — for example in the 1907 bear market and again in 1919 when he secretly bought all the stocks in cotton. His most notable trade was during the 1929 Great Depression. He amassed huge short positions in anticipation of the great bear market. He made over $100 million in that period and got a nickname for it — the Great Bear of Wall Street.

## Ray Dalio

Ray was born (in 1949) in the Jackson Height neighborhood of Queen's borough in New York City. His father was a jazz musician. He obtained an undergraduate degree in finance from Long Island

University, and in 1973, he earned an MBA from Harvard Business School.

He started investing as a kid. When he was 12, he bought shares of Northeast Airlines for $300, which later tripled in value when the company merged with another firm. After graduation, he traded commodity futures on the floor of the New York Stock Exchange and later became the Director of Commodities at Dominick & Dominick LLC.
Dalio would also work at Shearson Hayden Stone as a broker and futures trader before founding Bridgewater Associates, an investment management company, in 1975. The firm took off in his two-bedroom apartment in New York City and would continue operating from there until 1981, when it acquired an office in Westport, Connecticut.

Mr. Dalio and his firm enjoyed early success but also encountered some hiccups along the way, which made him modify his investment approach. In 2005, Bridgewater Associates became the largest hedge fund in the world. By the end of 2017, the firm had over $160 billion in assets. His personal net worth as of 2019 was over $18.4 billion.

Ray Dalio has authored several books, including How the Economic Machine Works, A Template for Understanding Big Debt Crises, and Principles, which was Amazon's #1 business book of 2017 and a New York Times #1 best-seller. He has spent over $760 million in philanthropy through his Dalio Foundation. The Foundation supports inner-city education, nature conservation, polio eradication, and microfinance.

# Chapter Five

# Trading Psychology

"Trading is 10% buying, 10% selling and 80% waiting"

If you wanna become a successful trader, the first thing you should be do- ing is having a clear mindset. If you did a mistake, you should write it down and learn what you did wrong. You should be trading with a good mood and a plan. Mood plays a very big role when it comes to trading and having a stable mood is a must. In addition to rating your general mood, it's also important to identify feelings of regret and revenge. When we have made a series of losing trades, we regret it. Regret is a powerful emotion; it is often more powerful than fear and greed. Traders have a strong need to avoid regret. Feeling regret forces us to admit that we were wrong. It makes us feel guilty. We entertain "if-only" scenarios: "If only I had done X or Y, I would not have lost." Regret makes us feel inadequate and uncomfortable.

The easiest way to avoid regret is to deny you have made a mistake, to believe that one can still make back what one has lost. The problem with avoiding regret is that you shift your attention away from the problem. You don't notice that something is wrong. You fail to see that a fundamental factor has changed, either you have changed psychologically or the mar- ket conditions have changed. In either case, it is better to stand aside than continue trading. Look for signs that you are avoiding regret. Focus on feelings of anger, frustration, or revenge. When you have made a series of losses that you view as unfair, you will feel angry; you will want to take your revenge out on the markets. When you feel these emotions, it' is probably a way of avoiding subsequent feelings of regret upon admitting a loss.  It is vital for your survival to stop trading at that point. You have lost your objectivity and it is likely that you will trade impulsively because your full attention is not on your immediate experience. A related emotion is a fear.

When you are afraid of the consequences of losing money, you are also avoiding regret. It is better to stop trading, regain your composure, and start up again when you are refreshed, which may be the next day. You should also take active steps to minimize feelings of regret. Neutralize these emotions by monitoring your self-talk.

When one feels regret, he or she usually thinks, "I should have done X, and I'm an unworthy person for not doing X." The truth, however, is that the markets are unpredictable. You can't blame yourself for not anticipating every possible influence that may go against your trading strategy.

And if you lost money because you didn't clearly specify a trading plan or stick with it, feeling regret is not going to help you very much. It may be useful in this case to kick yourself a little, but it is much more useful to take a more positive outlook, and think, "Trading takes practice; the more I practice, the more I will develop the discipline I need to be a profitable trader." By acknowledging that you have made a little mistake and remind- ing yourself that you will do everything possible to minimize its significance, you will feel less regret. You can acknowledge your limitations more easily. But, whatever you do, don't dig the hole deeper. Face your limitations, regain your composure, and go back in when your mindset and mar- ket conditions are just right. You will find that you will make more profits in the long run.

Trading can be frustrating at times. You put in a heroic effort, but it doesn't always pay off in the way that you had hoped. When you finally do win big, you naturally want to celebrate. You may even get a "swelled head," and feel invincible as if you are on top of the world. Why not celebrate? You deserve it. It is healthy to occasionally pat yourself on the back for a job well done, but don't get too full of yourself. There are many tales of expert, skilled traders who were at the top of the field and the idol of many, but due to changes in the markets, they ended up busted. Just when everything seems to be going well, market conditions change, and methods that once brought in steady profits suddenly stop working. That's why seasoned traders suggest staying humble. You must stay humble, and focused on continually honing your trading skills in anticipation of the next major change in the markets. A humble approach to trading will help you stay calm and focused.  Getting a swelled head often interferes with maintaining a calm, objective, and unemotional mindset. Basking in the glory of success can be intoxicating. You may start to think you are invincible as if you can't lose. You may then start bragging to your friends about how well you are doing, or start spending money extravagantly. When that happens, it may be the start of your demise. In a subtle way, you will start to put extra pressure on yourself to perform up to especially high standards that are almost impossible to maintain. You will try to keep up your reputation. You may dread failure because should you fail, you will have to admit to yourself and friends that you were not as invincible as you had claimed. At that point, you will have trouble staying objective. And once that happens, it is bound to impact your trading. The added pressure to perform, along with the psychological need to save face, will take a toll on your limited psychological resources. You will have less energy to focus on your trading, and you will likely make trading mistakes that will lead to your downfall.

It is important to keep your ego out of trading. Don't build yourself up, but don't overly criticize or condemn yourself either. Stay realistically upbeat and focus on developing your skills as a trader. Work toward excellence, not perfection. You have to be good, but not perfect. You must have top-notch trading skills, but you don't need to be the best trader in history. When you take your ego out of the picture and stay modest, you will find it easier to concentrate. And when you focus on the process of trading, rather than the prize, you will trade more profitably.

Trading with discipline is one of the greatest challenges for traders. It is common to hear novice traders say that they just can't help but abandon their trading plan. It's understandable. One may carefully devise a trading plan and have every intention of following it, but when it comes to actually put money on the line, they have trouble doing it. For some people, it may just be a matter of the stress of having to face a potential loss. But for others, discipline takes considerable effort. It's easy to understand why. Trading is a lot like playing sports. It is a good idea to have a plan, but it doesn't seem to make sense to follow it rigidly. It is often necessary to make midcourse corrections. That is why finding the proper level of discipline is a challenge. You don't want to trade too sporadically, but on the other hand, you don't want to be too inflexible and over-disciplined.

Some people have no trouble with discipline. They like rules and enjoy fol- lowing them. Other people, in contrast, dislike rules and structure. They are independent-minded and live by their own rules. Traders tend to be in the latter group. They aren't afraid of taking a risk or going their own way. These traits are ideal for trading profitably, but on the other hand, they aren't particularly consistent with a disciplined trading style. At times, those attracted to trading may have trouble maintaining discipline.

If you have trouble with discipline and are a little impulsive, you can learn to develop more self-control and discipline. First, keep in mind that you don't have to be disciplined all the time. You only need to be disciplined when you are putting on a trade. It sometimes helps to remember this fact. It eases some of the pressure to think that you only need to be focused when you make specific trades, rather than during all waking hours. Second, it is essential to outline a very detailed trading plan. You should specify exactly what signals tell you to enter a trade, and what signals tell you to exit. Some traders make the mistake of leaving some of these factors unspecified, figuring they can just extemporize when the time comes. But this approach presents problems for discipline. When you don't know what to do specifically, you will be sloppy and less likely to maintain self- control. Third, it is important to make sure your energy level is high, yet your stress level is low. Psychological resources are required to maintain self-control and discipline. When you are tired and worn out, you have lit- tle energy left over to focus on managing your trade. To keep your peak performance edge, it's vital to make sure you are relaxed, rested, and energized. If you aren't, you'll tend to make careless mistakes. Discipline is vital for trading success. It is essential that you develop a sense of discipline. The more disciplined you can trade, the more profits you'll realize.

**Here is a short story about a guy called John who did kick himself for making an obvious trading mistake.**

John is kicking himself right now. He just made an unexpected losing trade and he feels especially down. He expected to make a killing, and he was looking forward to winning and celebrating big. He thought he had done everything to prepare for the trade. He had looked at the moving average to discern the trend. He looked at the highs and lows of the stock for the past two months and set his stop loss accordingly. But in his strong desire to believe that he was about to execute a winning trade, he made a fatal error: He forgot to account for an upcoming earnings report. The company failed to meet analysts' forecasts, and the stock fell hard and fast. John didn't lose too much. His protective stop saved him, but it still hurts. He had gotten his hopes up, and now, he is especially disappointed.

John's plight is common for both seasoned and novice traders alike. There is a strong human need for eternal optimism. John isn't naïve. He knows that earnings reports can unexpectedly impact a stock price, but he had wanted to make a big winning trade so desperately that his unconscious mind prevented him from seeing matters clearly. Sometimes, we want something so strongly that we see things that just are not there, or we shut out things that we don't want to see. That's what John did. He didn't look carefully at all possibilities and he missed the obvious.

Why does John feel so badly? It could be for a number of reasons. First, he got his hopes up, but his dreams were dashed. When we expect a big win and don't get it, we are especially hurt. Second, John may be trying to live up to his own unrealistic, perfectionistic standards. He may be beating himself up because he wrongly believes that he must trade to perfection; he must account for all possibilities. It is a fact that had he been able to see that an earnings report was scheduled, an obvious potentially adverse event, he would have saved precious trading capital. But mistakes do hap- pen.

We are human. We often let our emotions take over, and when that happens, our rational mind doesn't stand a chance.

How can John feel better? He needs to change his frame of reference. When many people make an obvious mistake, they let their superego rule. Our superego consists of the ideals we strive for and the moral rules that our parents taught us while we were youngsters. When many people make a mistake, they treat the situation as if a parent or teacher were scolding them for breaking a rule. They re-experience feelings from childhood, hurt, beaten feelings. In some cases, the feelings may be shame or guilt. This is the wrong frame of reference to use to understand trading setbacks, how- ever.

When you lose money on a trade, it is not useful to allow your unconscious to equate the loss with being punished by your parents for breaking a rule. Instead, it is vital to look at matters from the perspective of a trader. Traders are human and they make mistakes. How many people actually make a living as a full-time, active trader? Hardly any. If you work under the assumption that anyone can trade, you will feel bad when you make a trading error. However, if you work under the assumption that few people can actually trade profitably, you'll quickly forgive yourself for making a mistake or a losing trade.

Every trader makes mistakes. There is a lot of information to sift through, and as we all know, our zealous pursuit of money often gets in the way of our ability to see the markets with crystal clear accuracy. When you change your frame of reference, your entire perspective changes. You stop getting your hopes up. When you remind yourself how challenging trading really is, you really start to recall that any given trade has little relevance in the context of a larger set of trades, and thus, it is unreasonable to expect success on a single trade. If you don't get your hopes up too high, you cannot be knocked down too far when a trade turns out to be a loser.

And when you realize that trading is so difficult that few people can trade the markets with perfection, you will accept your limitations and appreciate the winning trades you do make, instead of beating yourself self up for making the losing trades that are commonplace in the trading world.

The fear of missing out usually occurs when a stock is a making a big move and you missed it. This can lead to chasing an entry which is never a good trading decision because you will end up with a poor entry price and as you are caught up in the though of missing out you forget to manage your trade and risk.

The fear of missing out is driven by a desire to be a part of a good thing, even when all signs suggest that it is not a wise investment.

FOMO is so pernicious because we see other people succeeding, even if they are taking unjustifiable risks to do so, and we have a natural urge to join in. The more wildly successful other people are, which is usually direct- ly correlated with the amount of risk they are taking on, the stronger the urge to join in.

FOMO is usually harder for new traders to grasp because they haven't been burned as many times as someone who has been trading the markets for a while. The best way to deal with FOMO is to have rules in place and if you break them then you need to have some kind of punishment like no trading for the rest of the day.

You can't make trading decisions based on emotions no matter how much money you see other traders making on a crazy run. There will always be other opportunities so stick to your rules!

**No Fear!**

Fear is a broad sense of unjustified panic that occurs when market participants as a whole take a generally pessimistic view toward the financial, economic and political future.

Under a climate of fear, traders focus on and amplify any bad news, and are quick to close out long positions or open new short positions.

A climate of fear in the markets is self-reinforcing: as more people become afraid and sell, the greater the overall sense of fear becomes.

Under a climate of fear it is very difficult for an individual investor to make rational investing decisions based on reasonable expectations of the behavior of the market as a whole.

Fear is common in traders because we don't know what's going to happen after we enter a trade.

**Greed Is Good...Or Is It?**

Greed is the other side of the coin to fear. Greed is also similar to the fear of missing out, but more focused on a broader outlook instead of some smaller segment of the market. Under greed, economic, political and financial news is viewed extremely optimistic, and bad news is ignored of waved-away as unimportant. Greed creates a self-reinforcing cycle of rising asset prices and positive outlooks.

Traders become so accustomed to rising asset prices, that they begin to ignore obvious signs of risk or negative outcomes.

Trying to squeeze every last penny out of a move is a surefire way to give up profits and even lose money. The best way to handle greed is just like how you would handle fear. Set predetermined profit targets and when they hit, cash in! It's not rocket science you just have to be disciplined enough to follow your rules!

## Hope

Hope in trading psychology is the unrealistic expectation of something good happening. Traders can be hopeful at the height of a gain or the lows of a loss, but in all cases their desire for something to happen trumps their ability to rationally foresee outcomes.

Hope is a very natural human emotion, particularly in matters involving chance, risk and odds. The mere desire to want to believe in something is often enough to cloud our judgment and lead us to make poor decisions based on the hope that things will turn our way.

### How to Master Your Emotions

While mastering your emotions in trading is a never-ending battle, the basic framework for tackling the problem is actually quite simple.

Your emotions run wild when they are given the space to dominate your thinking, which is why professional traders always use a strict trading system that helps to contextualize their decisions and keep their emotions in check. Traders can rely on a tried and tested trading strategy to help them gauge and control their emotional state.

A regimented trading system offers an anchor of proven reason that traders can rely upon when attempting to interpret market information and their own emotions. Any effective trading strategy is composed of various rules that help to frame all investment decisions.

## Rules for Identifying Trades

The rules for identifying trades are useful for keeping traders on track and focused on those areas where their knowledge and experience gives them an advantage.

These rules are particularly useful when it comes to controlling for greed and the fear of missing out, as it keeps traders in a safe area that they understand instead of chasing profits in asset classes that are alien to them.

It's weird to say, but you need to be like a robot when trading. You have to be systematic and rely on your trading process and rules to be your guidelines for success.

## Rules for Executing Trades

The actual opening and closing of positions is always the most difficult and stressful aspect of trading. Even the most well-researched trades can go poorly if the trader is overly emotional when executing trades.

Having a set of strict rules for how and when to execute trades is essential to maximizing the profits from good ideas and minimizing the losses from trades gone wrong. An extensive use of advanced orders, such as profit-takers and stop orders, is an important element of a strong trade execution system.

When I first started trading, if I broke any of my rules I would have to stop trading for the day and make myself review my trading process. Eventually I broke my rules less and my trading improved. Now every once and a while I will break a rule but I have the experience and know-how to correct it and get back on track.

## Rules After You Trade

Whether you just met your weekly profit target in one trade or wiped out two day's worth of work, it is always wise to have a system for cooling down after one trade before moving on to the next.

Every trade will color your emotional state, so the best traders know how to cleanse themselves of the lingering emotions of the last trade before moving on to the next one.

## Master Your Emotions

While many traders may be technically skilled, the greatest traders are masters of personal discipline first and trading knowledge second.

A knowledge of the common pitfalls in trading psychology and a strict set of rules for trading are both essential to achieving lasting success in trading. With these in place, it is simply a matter of putting in the time and effort to become the master of your emotions and a master of trading.

I think trading is the only place in life where I can say I am totally responsible for my outcomes...That's huge in a world where previously waiting on someone else to make decisions about my income felt like a prison. I now have full autonomy.  We have an idea of what will happen but we don't know this with 100% certainty and when you have a lot of money on the line and don't know what's going to happen, it can cause fear and anxiety.

A good to way to counterbalance fear is by trading within your means and setting an acceptable loss amount. This way you know, before you even enter the trade, that you are only risking a certain amount.

This takes some of the uncertainty out of the trading process because now we know what is on the line. Every time I enter a trade, I tell myself that I may lose money and that's OK, just don't lose more than my predetermined amount!

Another way fear gets in our way is when we are trading with too much size that it makes us uncomfortable and fearful of losing too much money or even worse, blowing up our account. That's why sizing is so important.

Start off small and gradually work yourself up to larger size. Just because you had a solid month doesn't mean you should go from trade 500 shares to 5,000 shares.

# Final Thoughts

First, throw out your crystal ball and educate yourself. Hone your skills with practice and study. No one can predict with 100% certainty the future price moves of an equity. What you can do however, is make an educated guess about the general direction of a stock's price and about its floor or ceiling. You have to understand the company that you plan to trade and admitted- ly, that takes a lot of time and effort.

There are different ways to make educated predictions about a company's stock price but a prerequisite to any strategy is understanding the company itself. What is the company's product and who are its competitors? What is its market position? What are its strengths and weaknesses? Does it have a competitive moat that makes it difficult for new competitors to enter the market? Are there any significant risks? Who are the leaders and are they invested in the company or are they stringing it out?

Next, look to the future. Some traders use charts to help them gauge future price movements which means studying and learning chart patterns and how they pertain to the industry your chosen equity is in. How has the stock moved in the past in response to events such as earnings? While past performance is no guarantee of future results (sound familiar?), a lot of algorithmic trading programs make automatic decisions based on chart patterns and price movements so the charts can influence a stock's price. This effect is likely more pronounced for short-term or event-driven movements and therefore might be more relevant to shorter-term options strategies.

Other traders use fundamental analysis to guide their future expectations. You should learn to read quarterly financial statements. You do not need to be a CPA or even take an accounting class, but you should at least know enough to get an idea of important factors like a company's free cash flow, debt, margins, and so on. What you want is to get a fairly accurate idea of a company's intrinsic value. In other words, what is a fair value, or price, for the company's stock? There are other factors that influence a stock's price such as sentiment, news stories and so on, but establishing a fair value provides you with some soft guardrails for the stock's price.

Once you have a fair-value price, you can use an appropriate options strategy based on your level of acceptable risk. Instead of guessing or get- ting a "hot tip" from a friend or hyped-up website, use your own brain and knowledge to make reasonable estimates. (This is not to say that you have to do it all on your own; there are many reputable websites where knowledgable analysts discuss both charting and fundamentals. There are also a variety of tools available to help you be more efficient in your research, charting, and trading.)

The second thing you should do is understand risk, both generally for options trading as well as specifically for each trade you put on. Different options strategies have different risk profiles. Selling naked puts is riskier than buying long calls. With the former, you are on the hook to buy 100 shares of the underlying equity if the stock's price is below your put's strike price. For each contract, you are at risk for however much 100 shares costs at the strike price, minus the premium you received when you sold the contract. If the stock goes to zero, you lose the entire amount. On the other hand, the most you risk with a long call is the premium that you paid for it, so don't spend more than you're willing to lose. The bottom line is, know the risk profile of each strategy you use.

There is more to risk than simply how much you stand to lose on a single position, and the odds of that loss. You can think of that as positional risk, but you also need to factor in portfolio risk. Many options strategies, including selling naked options, require using buying power (or margin) in your account. Calculating buying power is beyond the scope of this article, but suffice it to say that if you over-extend your buying power and the market turns against your positions, you might face a margin call in which your brokerage sells your positions without your consent or participation. This is a worst-case scenario as it often means your stocks are sold out from under you at the worst possible time such as during a correction. When you use buying power, your entire portfolio is potentially at risk, so use caution and limit naked (short) options to a small portion of your over- all options trading.

Finally, have a plan and stick to it; do not trade on emotion. This is likely the hardest element to master. Know ahead of time what your exit point is for each strategy and position. It is fine to adjust your fair-value estimates for your positions, especially the longer-term options where conditions might change. But don't panic when your positions go negative for a day or a week or a month. Most options strategies can be rolled out or ex- tended and if you did your research, you should be confident in your price expectation. If you managed and spread out your risk, then a few bad positions should not affect your overall long-term performance.

Also, be patient. By definition, options positions have an expiration date. Choosing that date is part of your research and is one of the factors in your plan. Try to avoid changing up the plan mid-stream unless there are very good, rational reasons for doing so. Getting excited or depressed because the position does not seem to be playing out the way you expected is neither rational nor a good reason to bail on the position. You do not need to look at multi-month positions every day. Check in once a week or so, but be patient. Give your positions time to play out, and when you are wrong, learn from it and apply your knowledge to your future positions.

Over time you will get more experience and have more successful closed positions.